SIMPLE SMOKING

SIMPLE SMOKING

Over 80 Recipes for the Home-Smoking Enthusiast

Paul Kirk

Skyhorse Publishing

Copyright © 2001, 2011 Quintet Publishing Limited
This book produced by Quantum Publishing Ltd., 6 Blundell Street, London N7 9BH

Skyhorse Publishing books may be purchased in bulk at special discounts for sales promotion, corporate gifts, fund-raising, or educational purposes. Special editions can also be created to specifications. For details, contact the Special Sales Department, Skyhorse Publishing, 307 West 36th Street, 11th Floor, New York, NY 10018 or info@skyhorsepublishing.com.

www.skyhorsepublishing.com

10 9 8 7 6 5 4 3 2 1

Library of Congress Cataloging-in-Publication Data is available on file.

ISBN: 978-1-61608-317-5

Printed in China

CONTENTS

Introduction

SMOKING IS enjoying a revival all over the world. With this book you will be able to learn the principles governing it and join in the fun. Try your hand at stovetop smoking or smoke your own bacon or a whole salmon. You may even be inspired to build an old-fashioned walk-in smokehouse. As you gain confidence, you will be able to experiment with different flavors and devise your own recipes, creating rubs and marinades using your favorite combination of herbs and spices.

Smoking is essentially a means of preserving meat or fish by exposing it to the aromatic smoke of burning hardwood, usually after pickling in salt or brine. Why smoke foods? Historically, smoking came about through necessity. With no refrigeration or canning procedures developed, people found brining and curing an effective means of preserving their food. We can safely speculate that the process came about by happy accident, when a cave man concealed some meat on a ledge above the fire he burned to cook on and forgot about it for some days or weeks. When he or someone else eventually came upon it they found it to be dry and smoked and not rotten.

Historical references to smoke-cooking abound. There is a barbecue or smoking pit in central China, for example, which is reported to be more than 5000 years old. Sausages, which the Romans referred to as *salus*,

Left *Seasoning your food before smoking helps give it a really distinctive flavor.*

Below *A simple salad or grilled vegetables are the perfect accompaniment to a spicy smoked chicken dish.*

Right *Paul Kirk (far left) and his team prepare for a cookout.*

meaning salted or preserved, are mentioned in Babylonian records dating from 1500 B.C. and Homer refers to blood sausage in 900 B.C. A Cypriot text dating from the fifth century B.C. refers to salami, and the Italian method of cooking in wood fired ovens is well documented in history. To this day a great delicacy in Iceland is smoked lamb, which is cured then buried in the ground to mature. In South Africa they still produce sun-dried meat called biltong, and in many countries dried salt cod is used as a base for many interesting and traditional dishes. As methods have become more defined, hot smoking has progressed to smoke roasting and nowadays there are all manner of smokers and techniques to choose from when cooking your food in this way.

The primary function of brines nowadays is to enhance the flavor of meat or fish rather than preserve it. With an increasingly varied store of ingredients now available to us world-wide, and global influences in cooking and flavoring, the opportunity to create revolutionary smoking sensations is too good to miss. The examples of brining and curing included in this book are not the traditional brines that were more concerned with preserving than flavoring, and were often a hit-and-miss business because people kept no records of how they had made the brine and were not too specific about quantities.

Enrich your culinary repertoire by exploring this exciting area of cooking and remember that it is not as laborious as it might sound. Smoke-cooking is essentially a simple art that relies on good-quality ingredients to produce a delicious result. Have fun and enjoy!

Smoking Know-how

S MOKE-COOKING is not as complicated as it sounds. Start with the best
ingredients you can find so that you get great results every time. Have
patience and document what you do, step by step. This is not as
laborious as it might seem. Finally, enjoy what you are doing and have fun.

When I was first introduced to the world of smoking it was twofold—
part preserving and part flavoring. Today it is mostly done for flavor. The
recipes in this cookbook are for flavor and enjoyment, not preserving. Even
the bacon recipe needs to be refrigerated after curing and smoking. Smoke
helps preserve food, but it is primarily used to enhance the flavor of the food.

Smoke is usually generated by a heat source, charcoal, gas, electricity, or
wood. In smoke-cooking the smoky flavor comes from hardwoods, each of
which produces a slightly different flavor. Hickory is one of the most popular.
Some of the other woods you can choose from are apple, cherry, oak, maple,
alder, mesquite, nut, and aged fruitwoods; peach, plum, pear, and orange
also work well. Usually the hardwood that is indigenous to your area is your
best bet to start with. Greenwood burns at a higher temperature and for a
longer time than aged wood (that is, wood that has been cut and dried for at
least 6 months). It also provides more smoke.

Left *Turning the meat during
cooking is important to help
distribute the smoked flavor evenly.*

Below *The results speak for
themselves with this spicy chili-
rubbed rack of lamb (see page 68).*

COOKING-WOOD CHART

WOOD TYPE	CHARACTERISTICS	USE WITH
Acacia	Mesquite family/strong	Most meat, vegetables
Alder	Delicate with a hint of sweetness	Fish, pork, poultry, game birds, and salmon
Almond	Nutty and sweet smoke flavor, light ash	Good for all meat
Apple	Slightly sweet but dense, fruity smoke flavor	Beef, poultry, game birds, pork, and ham
Apricot	Milder and sweeter flavor than hickory	Good for most meat
Ash	Fast-burning, light but distinctive flavor	Good for fish and red meat
Birch	Medium-hard wood with a flavor similar to maple	Good for pork and poultry
Cherry	Slightly sweet, fruity smoke flavor	Good for all meat
Cottonwood	Very subtle flavor	Good for most meats
Grape Vines	Aromatic, similar to fruitwoods	Good for all meat
Grapefruit	Medium smoke flavor with a hint of fruit	Excellent for beef, pork, and poultry
Hickory	Pungent, smoky, baconlike flavor. The most common wood used	Good for all smoking especially pork and ribs
Lemon	Medium smoke flavor with a hint of fruit	Excellent for beef, pork, and poultry
Lilac	Very light, subtle with a floral hint	Good for seafood and lamb
Maple	Mild, smoky, somewhat sweet flavor	Good for pork, poultry, cheese, vegetables, and small game birds
Mesquite	Strong earthy flavor	Most meat, especially beef, and most vegetables
Mulberry	Sweet applelike aroma	Beef, poultry, game birds, pork, and ham
Nectarine	Milder and sweet, flavor than hickory	Good for most meat

WOOD TYPE	CHARACTERISTICS	USE WITH
Oak	The second most common wood used. Heavy smoke flavor. Red oak is considered the best by many pitmasters	Good for red meat, pork, fish, and game
Orange	Medium smoke flavor with a hint of fruit	Excellent for beef, pork, and poultry
Peach	Slightly sweet flavor	Good for most meat
Pear	Slightly sweet flavor	Poultry, game birds, and pork
Pecan	More like oak than hickory, but not as strong	Good for most meat
Plum	Milder and sweeter than hickory	Good for most meat
Walnut	Very heavy smoke flavor, usually mixed with lighter wood like pecan or apple. Can be bitter if used alone or not aged	Good for red meat and game

EQUIPMENT

You don't have to spend a lot of money if you don't want to. You can make a smoker out of any barbecue grill or pit that has a cover or lid so long as you can control the temperature.

You need to be able to control the airflow to the heat source if it is charcoal, wood, or a free-burning combustible product. Gas and electricity are usually controlled by means of valves and switches. Control is the ability to adjust the air supply going in (if fire has no oxygen it can't burn) as well as the air escaping, venting, or exhausting. The exhaust control is where you regulate how much smoke will be kept in the food chamber. Restricting or increasing the airflow controls the burning of the charcoal and hardwood.

You should use the wood or smoldering agent in conjunction with your heat source. A smoldering agent could be wood, fresh or dried herbs, rice, tea, or sugar (all three are used in the Tea-smoked duck recipe).

The smoking (food) chamber is where you place anything you want to smoke. It is usually located between the smoke generator and the exhaust.

A standard kettle barbecue is an easy way to cook smoked food when you are just starting out.

The list of cookers or smokers I have cooked on is long and varied, and includes several homemade models.

A gas grill can be used as a smoker if it has dual burners or controls.

Water smokers are usually powered by electricity or charcoal and have a domed lid, food grates, a pan for holding water, and a heat source on the base. They are great for cooking foods that benefit from added moisture.

Free-standing smokehouses are another option, whether homemade or commercial. The latter range from those that will accommodate 4 large rolling racks with 5 or more smoking chambers. Catering

Below This large free-standing smoker is for serious smokers who enjoy a good cookout.

Above *The Smoky Mountain Smoker is a compact portable cooker which is large enough to accommodate a sizeable chicken or rack of ribs.*

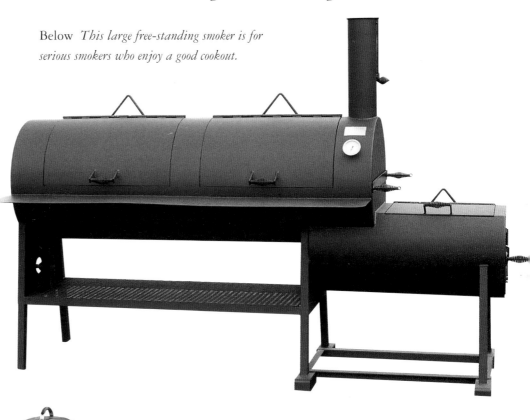

smoking units are extremely expensive but enable you to control the heat, smoke, and humidity with absolute stability.

Setting up a small cooker to be an indirect cooker or smoker is easy. Bank your charcoal briquettes to one side, (the manufacturer will tell you to bank coals on both sides of the cooker and use a water pan). What and how long you are cooking will determine the amount of charcoal you will need to use. Count how many briquettes you start with for a particular dish, keep track of the number and make a note of it for future reference. Light the charcoal, following the manufacturer's instructions. Avoid petrochemicals if at all possible.

This gas grill can be used to smoke food and will be sufficient to feed a small party or family gathering.

Hot Smoking and Stovetop Smoking Techniques

HOT SMOKING is a more traditional technique, not as widely practiced as it used to be, most having moved on to smoke-roasting or barbecuing, which is done at a higher temperature. When I am going to hot-smoke, I pick something young, tender, and succulent that will cook in 4 to 5 hours or less. You can hot-smoke for as long as you wish but I prefer to keep to this time. You must take care to keep the meat moist by using a baste, which can be a reserved marinade, a concoction of your devising, or just apple juice. Melted butter makes a good baste and it is one of the best flavor enhancers you can use. I start basting halfway through the cooking process. Turn your piece of meat at this time, then baste. Repeat the basting process after a further hour and at regular intervals thereafter, as the recipe dictates. Avoid opening the smoker during the cooking time to check how the meat is doing. When you open up the smoker you can lose precious heat, smoke, and temperature. Only open your smoker to turn the meat, baste, or put something else on the smoker.

Stovetop smoking is good if you want a light smoke flavor and are cooking for a short time. If you are using a stovetop smoking kit, sprinkle ½ to 1 cup of sawdust in the bottom of a Dutch oven. Place the rack over the sawdust. Place the Dutch oven on a burner over a high heat. When the sawdust starts to smolder, place the salmon on the rack, cover with the lid, and reduce the heat to medium. Cook for 20 to 30 minutes or until the fish flakes easily. Don't open the Dutch before the 20 minutes. Keeping a log can be really helpful: you can develop your own stovetop smoking times and temperature charts. I have done boneless, skinless chicken breasts, using the timing above. For a whole chicken, I smoke it on the stovetop Dutch oven until it stops smoking. Then place the chicken in a preheated oven and cook at 350°F for about 45 minutes, until it is done and has a pleasantly smoked flavor.

Commerical stainless-steel stovetop smokers, consisting of a 15 × 11 × 3¼-inch pan with a wire rack and a slide-on lid, are used the same way as Dutch-oven stovetop smokers. You could also use a broiler pan with a wire rack to keep the meat or vegetables above the sawdust or wood chips. Cover with heavy-duty aluminum foil. If the pan and rack are not deep enough to make a domed X-shaped "tent," use spring-type wire, bending it between the opposite corners.

Above *Flavored marinades can be used to baste the meat during cooking as well as to impart flavor before.*

Right *Hot smoking can be done on a conventional kettle barbecue in the backyard, so get your coals heated and get smokin!*

Smoke-roasting Techniques

SMOKE-ROASTING or barbecuing, is becoming increasingly popular all over the world. All smoking—cold- and hot smoking, smoke-roasting or barbecuing is done by indirect cooking. The fire is away from the meat or fish. Barbecuing is generally defined as slow-cooking meat with or over the heat of hardwood and/or charcoal at a temperature of 200 to 375°F.

The first thing to do before smoke-roasting is to set up the smoker. The most readily available is the kettle type, with a lid. Have a thermometer on hand, a candy/deep-fry one is ideal, calibrated from 50 to 450°F. To test your thermometer for accuracy, place it in boiling water: it should read 212 °F. You also need a cork; I like to use a champagne cork. Drill a hole in the cork about the same size as the barrel of the thermometer. Insert the thermometer barrel through the hole in the cork and it will cradle in the vent hole of the smoker lid, without the barrel touching the lid itself, enabling you to get a true temperature reading.

I prefer lump or natural charcoal to charcoal briquettes, but beginners generally find briquettes easier to start with because they burn more evenly

Below *Use the air vent to control the heat.*

Above *This pork tenderloin (see page 59) has been spiced up with chiles and ginger for a real flavor kick.*

Above right *Be careful when turning fish that is nearly done as it can come apart; use a large spatula or fish slice.*

than natural lump charcoal. Avoid petroleum products, as these can taint the taste. You also need wood chunks or chips for flavor (see page 9).

I also suggest a water pan, which helps to retain moisture in your cooker at all times, but some people prefer not to use one. The object is to provide humidity in your smoker for the meat you are smoking. To achieve this, you can use a water pan, and baste with apple juice or cider, or dispense with the water pan and baste with a basting sauce. I use an old bread pan but you can use any pan that will work for you, bearing in mind, it should be large enough so you don't have to refill it every hour. The water pan does not necessarily have to be filled with water, but using wine, beer, apple juice, cider, or vinegar seems to make little or no difference to the flavor of the smoked meat.

Manufacturers usually recommend placing a water pan in the middle of the grill and charcoal fires on either side. In my opinion this restricts your cooking area. I put the fire on one side and the water pan on the other. This gives you the other three-quarters of the grill/smoker to work on. If you're cooking, you might as well fill the grill up; smoked meat freezes well.

Place your hot coals over an air vent if possible. This gives you better control of the heat by controlling the airflow. Place the water pan right up against the hot coals. Place the meat grill on the smoker, making sure that the handle-holes are directly over the hot coals. If you have a grill with flip-up grates that open on one or both sides then put them over the hot coals. Place the lid (cover) on the smoker with the vent holes opposite the hot coals. If you are smoking for more than 40 minutes to 1 hour replenish the cooker with hot coals and wood chunks as follows: place your thermometer in the vent holes. When the smoker temperature reaches 230 to 250°F or your desired cooking temperature, drop 2 wood chunks of your choice on the hot coals then place the meat on the smoker. Place the cover on the smoker and do not open it until it is time to turn or baste the meat.

If you are planning to smoke/cook for several hours you will need to add hot coals to maintain an even temperature. As a general rule the temperature will start to drop between 40 and 60 minutes. It takes between 20 and 30 minutes for hot coals to get ready, using a chimney. If you keep a note of all your smoking procedures as you complete them, you will know when to start some more coals in order to get them hot. I usually start with 40 to 50 briquettes. Cut that number in half when preparing hot coals to add to the smoker—this is enough to keep the smoker at temperature for another 40 to 60 minutes. Repeat the process for as long as you're cooking.

If you are using a water smoker you can fill the charcoal ring with charcoal. Light a chimney of charcoal, pour the hot coals on top of the raw charcoal, add a couple chunks of hardwood, and cover it, then bring it up to temperature by adjusting the air intake and the exhaust vent. This smoker is now set up to smoke for 10 to 12 hours. Replenish the water in the water pan, turn your meat, and baste. If you are cooking with charcoal and wood you will get a smoke flavor. You can soak your wood and wood chips in water. This will give you more smoke and the fire will burn a little slower.

Below left Smoking adds a really unique and strong flavor to many varieties of fish

Below Smoke-roasting need not be restricted to meat-eaters — vegetables respond equally well to this method of cooking.

Seasoning Techniques

CURING

Meat and fish have been cured for many centuries using salt and smoke. In time the use of saltpeter (KNO_3, potassium nitrite), became popular, but this has now been replaced with sodium nitrite, sodium nitrate, and other compounds such as absorbic acid. Chemical compounds like absorbic acid are substances that are used primarily to preserve the color of the meat.

Much folklore surrounds the art of curing food, substitutes including the ancient belief that curing during the week of a full moon would ensure a better product that would be protected from all the elements. Procedures for curing range from packing the meat in salt and allowing it to cure for a suitable length of time. The meat was then placed or arranged on a wooden shelf or packed in a wooden box or barrel and stored in a cool, dark place, usually a cellar.

When my uncles Len and Chuck Le Cluyse cured pork bellies (bacon), usually 4 or 5 at a time, they would use about 8 pounds of noniodized sea salt for every 100 pounds of meat. They would mix the salt with 4 to 5 cups of molasses (1 cup per belly); 2 ounces of medium ground black pepper, and

Below Mops and dry spice rubs moisten and flavor the ingredients before and during the cooking process.

Bottom right The lime juice used in the marinade for this chicken dish is enhanced by a squeeze of fresh lime when you come to serve it.

2 ounces of cayenne. They smeared the mixture all over the bellies and placed the bellies in a special wooden chest they built just for the bacon. They would then weight the chest and put it in a large refrigerator where it would cure for 6 to 8 weeks. After this time they washed the cure off the bellies and hung them in their walk-in smokehouse. They would smoke it for 3 to 6 days at about 100 to 120°F. When I cure bacon I buy one belly weighing about 18 to 22 pounds. I cut it in half and square it up. I rub it with a brown sugar cure and place it in an oak box or a plastic container. Curing your own bacon is fun, and yields a much better product than you can buy commercially.

BRINING

In times gone by, brining meant dissolving salt in water until the solution would float a raw egg. The brine would usually be heated to get more salt into the solution, then allowed to cool. This brine would work well with turkey and salmon. Immerse the bird or fish in the solution and weight it down with a plate and a brick, keeping it under the top of the brine. Place it in the refrigerator for 4 to 6 days. Wash the brine from the meat and smoke it.

RUBS OR BARBECUE SEASONINGS

A barbecue seasoning or rub is a dry marinade. Season the meat and put it on the cooker or allow it to marinate for 2, 4, or 6 hours or overnight in the refrigerator. Dry rubs are my choice of seasoning for most of the hot, stovetop, smoke-roasting, and barbecue recipes I prepare. When making a rub I suggest equal parts of sugar and salt, (1 cup of each). I prefer white cane sugar to brown sugar, because the moisture in the brown sugar makes it tend to clump. For salt I prefer seasoned salt, garlic salt, celery salt, and onion salt. Next, I

Above *Ginger, cinnamon, peppercorns, garlic, lemon, and tumeric are just some of the seasonings you can use to flavor your smoked food.*

SEASONING CHART

TIMES IN HOURS

6 to 8	Spare ribs	Venison	Duck	
5 to 7	Beef roast	Beef brisket	Beef short ribs	Beef ribs
4 to 6	Beef kabobs	Beef steaks	Lamb kabobs	Game birds
4 to overnight	Turkey	Turkey quarters	Flank steak	Skirt steak
3 to 4	Pork tenderloin	Pork chops	Pork loin	
2 to 4	Chicken breasts	Chicken	Chicken portions	Chicken wings
½ to 2	Fish	Shellfish		

add some paprika for color, and equal parts of chili powder and black pepper; this recipe will handle 2 tablespoons of each. That is a basic barbecue rub. Now add your signature; pick 3 of your favorite spices or herbs you think will enhance the flavor of the meat you are about to smoke. If you can't decide, start with 1 teaspoon allspice, 1 teaspoon ground ginger, and 1/4 teaspoon ground cloves. If you like a little kick, add 1 teaspoon cayenne as well. This mixture will make an all-purpose seasoning or rub. To apply the rub sprinkle it on like salt and pepper rather than rubbing it into the meat or fish.

MARINADES

A marinade is a liquid mixture (usually a combination of an acid ingredient such as vinegar or lemon juice, oil, and seasonings) used to season meat or vegetables before cooking. The primary function of marinades is to flavor, moisten, and soften rather than to tenderize, as is commonly believed. If meat is left in a marinade too long it can make the outer muscle soft and mushy. On fish and boneless, skinless chicken breast, the acid can cook the flesh.

Below Flavoring oils with herbs, chiles, and garlic will add an extra dimension to your marinade.

SEASONING RECIPES

SEASONING, FROM MY perspective, is the most important chapter in this book. The more you know about seasonings, spices, and herbs the better cook you will be. I consider seasoning to be at the heart of smoked food cooking, so read through these recipes and make the best seasonings ever.

Cajun Seasoning

Yield about ¾ cup

½ cup paprika
2 Tbsp granulated garlic
1½ Tbsp cayenne
2 tsp dry mustard
2 tsp ground oregano
2 tsp seasoned salt
1 tsp ground thyme
1 tsp fine ground black pepper
1 tsp toasted ground cumin
1 tsp white pepper
½ tsp ground marjoram
½ tsp ground nutmeg

Combine the paprika, garlic, cayenne, mustard, oregano, seasoned salt, thyme, black pepper, cumin, white pepper, marjoram, and nutmeg in a sifter over a bowl and sift. Blend well. Store the seasoning in an airtight container in a cool dry place.

Caribbean Chicken Rub

Yield about 1 cup

¼ cup raw sugar
3 Tbsp kosher salt
1 Tbsp coarse ground black pepper
1 Tbsp lemon pepper
1 Tbsp orange pepper
1 Tbsp coarse ground allspice
1 Tbsp granulated garlic
1 Tbsp granulated onion
1 Tbsp coarse ground coriander
1 Tbsp dried orange zest, minced
2 tsp ground ginger

Combine the sugar, salt, black pepper, lemon pepper, orange pepper, allspice, garlic, onion, coriander, orange zest, and ginger in a bowl and blend well. Store in an airtight container in a cool dry place.

Barbecue Rub for Beef Brisket

Yield about 2½ cups

½ cup dried brown cane sugar
½ cup cane sugar
½ cup barbecue spice
½ cup paprika
¼ cup celery salt
2 Tbsp hickory salt
2 tsp black pepper
2 tsp celery seeds
1 tsp garlic powder
1 tsp cayenne

Combine the brown sugar, cane sugar, barbecue spice, paprika, celery salt, hickory salt, pepper, celery seeds, garlic powder, and cayenne in a bowl and blend well. Store in an airtight container in a cool dry place.

SMOKED PASTRAMI

Yield about 6 to 8 lb

2 quarts ice cold water (38 to 40°F)
2 oz mixed sodium nitrite and
    noniodized salt (available
    commercially)
1 Tbsp garlic juice
3½ oz sea or canning salt
1 oz dextrose powder
One 10-lb beef roast (lean brisket,
    or eye-of-round), trimmed
2 cups coarse ground black pepper
1 cup coarse ground coriander
1 cup dark brown sugar (optional)

Combine the water, sodium nitrite and noniodized salt mixture, garlic, salt, and dextrose powder in a bowl, stirring with a wire whisk to dissolve the seasonings.

Using a brine pump or a large syringe if you have one, fill your pump with the cure and pump generously onto the roast all over. Place the roast in a nonreactive container (a plastic one with a snap-on lid will work well), pour any excess cure over the roast, and keep submerged in the refrigerator for 3 to 5 days.

Combine the pepper, coriander, and sugar in a small bowl and blend well. Remove the roast from the cure and rub all sides with the pepper mixture, pressing it into the meat.

Place in a smoker preheated to 180°F with the dampers open. Cook for about 1 hour until the surface of the meat is dry. Close the dampers, about one-third, add smoking wood to the heat source and smoke at this temperature for 2 hours. Gradually increase the temperature to between 230 and 250°F, keeping a constant temperature until the internal temperature is between 175 and 180°F. Remove the meat and allow to cool to room temperature. Eat immediately or wrap and place in the refrigerator.

ALL-PURPOSE GAME MARINADE

Yield about 3 cups

¼ cup orange marmalade
¼ cup fresh lemon juice
¼ cup gin
¼ cup chicken or beef broth
¼ cup light soy sauce
1 Tbsp grated gingerroot
1 Tbsp juniper berries, crushed
1 Tbsp lemon zest
3 cloves garlic, minced
1 tsp dried basil
1 tsp black pepper
1½ cups olive oil

Combine the marmalade, lemon juice, gin, broth, ginger, juniper berries, lemon zest, garlic, basil, and pepper in a blender or food processor fitted with a steel blade. Process for 30 seconds to break up the marmalade. With the motor running slowly, pour in the oil in a steady stream until it is all incorporated. Make the marinade on the day you are using it for the best results.

Smoked Pastrami

BAY SEASONING

Yield about ½ cup

2 Tbsp powdered bay leaf
2 Tbsp celery salt
1 Tbsp dry mustard
2 tsp fine ground black pepper
1 tsp white pepper
1 tsp ground nutmeg
1 tsp ground ginger
1 tsp paprika
1 tsp cayenne
¾ tsp ground cloves
½ tsp ground cardamom

Combine the bay leaf, celery salt, dry mustard, black pepper, white pepper, nutmeg, ginger, paprika, cayenne, cloves, and cardamom. Blend well. Store in an airtight container in a cool dry place.

This seasoning can be used on almost any fish or seafood you want to smoke or grill. It is also good on chicken.

BROWN SUGAR/HONEY BACON CURE

Yield about 10 lb homemade smoked bacon

1 lb sea or canning salt (noniodized)
1 lb dark brown sugar
2 oz Praque powder No. 1 (sodium nitrite and noniodized salt, mixed with a ratio of 1:16)
2 cups honey
One 10 to 11-lb piece fresh pork belly

Combine the salt and the brown sugar with the sodium nitrite and noniodized salt mixture, and blend well. Rub the mixture all over the pork belly, (cut this into smaller pieces if desired) and place on a piece of plastic wrap or waxed paper. Spread the honey all over the pork belly, then seal in the wrap. Place in the refrigerator and allow to cure for about a week.

Remove the pork belly from the refrigerator and unwrap. Wash the excess honey and salt mixture with warm water. Pat dry with paper towels. Allow to rest for 30 minutes at room temperature. Place the pork in a smoker preheated to between 180 and 200°F with the dampers wide open. Dry the bacon for about 10 to 15 minutes. Add wood to your heat source, close the dampers about one-third, and reduce the temperature to about 150°F, smoking at that temperature until the internal temperature is between 127 and 130°F.

Reduce the temperature of the smoker to between 120 and 125°F until the pork belly reaches the color you desire. Remove, cover, and chill in the refrigerator overnight before slicing. Woods that work well for bacon are hickory and apple.

COACHES PORK PASTE

Yield about 4½ cups

1 cup cane sugar
½ cup dark brown cane sugar
½ cup seasoned salt
½ cup celery salt
½ cup paprika
¼ cup chili powder
2 Tbsp black pepper
2 Tbsp lemon pepper
2 tsp toasted ground cumin
1 tsp onion powder
1 tsp garlic powder
¼ to ½ cup olive oil
2 to 4 Tbsp white vinegar

Combine the cane sugar, brown sugar, seasoned salt, celery salt, paprika, chili powder, black pepper, lemon pepper, cumin, onion powder, and garlic powder in a bowl and blend well. Blend in the olive oil; use enough to form a texture that looks like wet sand. Add white vinegar a little at a time until the paste reaches the thickness you desire. Add more vinegar to form a thinner paste. Rub mixture all over your pork roast or ribs. Place in a plastic bag and allow to marinate for 4 to 5 hours in the refrigerator. Cook as desired, hot- or smoke-roasted. This paste will keep covered in a refrigerator for months.

POMEGRANATE MARINADE FOR CHICKEN

Yield about 3 cups

½ cup pomegranate juice or
   cranberry concentrate
½ cup orange juice
¼ cup fresh mint leaves
2 Tbsp Grand Marnier
1 Tbsp grated gingerroot
2 cloves fresh garlic, minced
1 tsp fresh ground black pepper
1 tsp sea salt
½ cup walnut oil
1 cup olive oil

Place the pomegranate juice, orange juice, mint, Grand Marnier, ginger, garlic, pepper, and salt in a blender fitted with a steel blade. Combine the walnut and olive oil in a pitcher. Process on high and add the oil in a steady stream until it is all blended. This marinade is best used on the day it is made.

ALL-MEAT MARINADE

Yield about 2⅓ cups

1¼ cups cider vinegar
¾ cup sunflower oil
2 Tbsp yellow mustard
1 Tbsp chili powder
1 Tbsp light brown cane sugar
1 Tbsp sea salt
1 tsp toasted ground cumin
1 tsp paprika
1 tsp fine ground black pepper
4 large cloves garlic, minced
1 to 2 Tbsp hot sauce

Combine the vinegar, oil, mustard, chili powder, sugar, salt, cumin, paprika, pepper, garlic, and hot sauce in a bowl, blending with a wire whisk. Best used on the day made.

SALMON BRINE

Yield about 1 gallon

1 lb brown sugar
1 cup sea or canning salt
1 cup soy sauce
1 cup dry white wine
1 tsp onion flakes
1 tsp granulated garlic
1 tsp white pepper
1 Tbsp Tabasco sauce or to taste
3 quarts water

Combine the brown sugar, salt, soy sauce, white wine, onions, garlic, white pepper, Tabasco sauce, and water in a bowl and blend well.

Cover the salmon with the brine, making sure that it is submerged; brine for 2 hours in the refrigerator or overnight. The unused brine will keep in the refrigerator for months. Remove the salmon from the brine and rinse with cold water. Season with whatever seasoning you like and smoke until the fish flakes easily.

Pomegranate Marinade

JERK SEASONING

Yield about ⅓ cup

2 Tbsp salt (noniodized)
1 Tbsp cane sugar
2 tsp ground Scotch Bonnet pepper
    or 1 tsp ground Scotch Bonnet
    pepper and 1 tsp cayenne
2 tsp granulated onion
2 tsp granulated garlic
1½ tsp ground allspice
1 tsp ground ginger
1 tsp fine ground black pepper
½ tsp ground cinnamon
¼ tsp ground cloves
¼ tsp ground nutmeg

Combine the salt, sugar, Scotch Bonnet pepper, onion, garlic, allspice, ginger, pepper, cinnamon, cloves, and nutmeg in a small bowl and blend well. Store in an airtight container in a cool dry place.

If you like the flavor of the Scotch Bonnet peppers but not all of the heat use 1 teaspoon Scotch Bonnet pepper and 1 teaspoon cayenne. It still has a good bite, but won't be as pungent. If you like more fire use 2 tablespoons of Scotch Bonnet pepper.

HONEY BRINE FOR TURKEY OR CHICKEN

Yield just over 1 gallon

1 cup canning or noniodized salt
1 cup dark brown sugar
½ cup liquid honey
1 Tbsp meat Morton Tender Quick
1 Tbsp white pepper
2 tsp ground ginger
2 tsp powdered bay leaf
1 tsp ground allspice
1 tsp ground clove
1 tsp mace
1 gallon water

Combine the salt, sugar, honey, Tender Quick, pepper, ginger, bay leaf, allspice, clove, mace, and water in a saucepan. Bring to a boil, stirring to dissolve the sugar and honey. Reduce the heat and simmer for about 15 minutes. Set aside and allow to cool.

Rinse your turkey or chicken with cold water. Place in a nonreactive container, pour the brine over the bird, and place a weight on the bird to hold it under the brine. Refrigerate for 4 to 8 hours or overnight. Rinse the bird with cold water and pat dry with paper towels. Season inside and out with your favorite rub or seasoning. Cook, smoke, then smoke-roast, barbecue, or deep-fry.

CHINESE BARBECUE SEASONING OR RUB

Yield about 1 cup

¼ cup cane sugar
2 Tbsp paprika
1 Tbsp dark brown sugar
1 Tbsp garlic salt
1 Tbsp seasoned salt
1 Tbsp celery salt
1 Tbsp onion salt
2 Tbsp chili powder
1 Tbsp fine ground Szechuan pepper
1 Tbsp fine ground black pepper
1 Tbsp dry mustard
2 tsp ground ginger
1 tsp Chinese five-spice powder
1 tsp cayenne

Combine the sugar, paprika, brown sugar, garlic salt, seasoned salt, celery salt, onion salt, chili powder, Szechuan pepper, black pepper, mustard, ginger, five-spice powder, and cayenne in a sifter and sift into a bowl. Blend well. Store in an airtight container in a cool dry place.

MEXICAN CHIPOTLE MARINADE

Yield about 1¾ cups

8 canned chipotle peppers in
    adobo sauce
2 Tbsp adobo sauce or tomato paste
1 cup fresh orange juice
¼ cup fresh lime juice
2 Tbsp red wine vinegar
1 Tbsp catsup
4 large cloves garlic, diced
One 3-in piece orange zest
1 tsp dried oregano
1 toasted ground cumin
1 tsp sea salt
1 tsp black pepper

Place the chipotles, adobo sauce, orange juice, lime juice, vinegar, catsup, garlic, orange zest, oregano, cumin, salt, and pepper in a saucepan. Bring to a boil. Reduce the heat to a vigorous simmer until the sauce is reduced by one third. Transfer to a blender fitted with a stainless steel blade, and purée until smooth. Allow to cool. This is a good marinade for pork and chicken. For the best flavor, use immediately.

RED WINE MARINADE FOR GAME

Yield about 3½ cups

2 cups red wine
¼ cup red wine vinegar
½ cup minced onion
½ cup minced carrot
4 to 6 cloves garlic, minced
2 bay leaves
2 tsp rubbed sage
1 tsp juniper berries, mashed
1 tsp whole cloves

Combine all the ingredients in a saucepan and bring to a boil. Reduce the heat and simmer for 30 minutes. Allow to cool before using. Marinate venison steaks for 3 to 4 hours and back strap and leg roast for 6 to 8 hours or overnight in the refrigerator.

HOT SMOKING AND STOVETOP SMOKING RECIPES

I FIRST BECAME interested in hot smoking at a very young age, watching my father, along with my grandfather and uncles practice the art. Cooking with wood and charcoal really is like learning an art or craft. There is also something special about cooking for your family, friends, employer, your church, or organization. As people enjoy the flavor of your smoked product (and you enjoy the praise!), you will achieve a real sense of accomplishment.

For anyone interested in getting into smoking, stovetop smoking is a great place to start. First, the equipment can cost next to nothing; you need a pan, a rack, wood chips or sawdust, and a tight fitting lid or cover, which can simply be a piece of metal or aluminum foil. Now for the sheer pleasure of it and a great learning experience, pick out one of the recipes and see how easy it is to start smoking.

CHICKEN WITH CHAMPAGNE SAUCE

Serves 8

Eight 5-oz boneless, skinless
   chicken breasts
3 Tbsp fresh lemon juice
1 Tbsp kosher salt
1 Tbsp fine ground black pepper
4 fresh peaches, peeled, pitted, and
   sliced thin

FOR THE SAUCE

1 stick sweet butter
1 cup minced red onions
¼ cup all-purpose flour
1 cup canned peaches, puréed
⅕ bottle Champagne
2 Tbsp peach schnapps

Sprinkle the chicken breasts with the lemon juice. Season with the salt and pepper and top with the peach slices. Place the chicken and peach on your cooker and smoke, using your favorite fruitwood, for 1 to 1½ hours.

In a saucepan over medium-hot heat add the butter and sauté the onions until soft but not browned. Blend in the flour and cook, stirring for 2 to 3 minutes. Do not let it brown. Stir in the peaches, Champagne, and schnapps and heat until the sauce has thickened. Spoon over the grilled chicken breasts and serve with spinach noodles.

SHANGHAI SMOKED CHICKEN

Serves 2 to 4

FOR THE MARINADE

½ cup soy sauce
2 Tbsp sunflower oil
2 Tbsp hoisin sauce
2 heaping Tbsp brown sugar
2 Tbsp sherry
1 Tbsp grated gingerroot
1 tsp sea salt
2 scallions, minced
1 tsp liquid smoke (optional)

One 3 to 4-lb whole chicken,
   butterflied

Combine the soy sauce, oil, hoisin, sugar, sherry, ginger, salt, scallions, and liquid smoke in a bowl and blend with a wire whisk.

Butterflying the chicken can be done with a paring knife. Place the chicken on its breast; cut down both sides of the backbone and remove. The only bones you have to cut are tiny rib bones. Open the chicken up, cut the piece of white gristle, and, placing your thumbs on either side of the breastbone, pull out the breastbone and the piece of white gristle at the base and back of the breast. Place the chicken in a large gallon-size zip-lock type plastic bag. Pour the marinade over the chicken and marinate for 2 to 4 hours in the refrigerator.

Remove the chicken from the marinade, place on your cooker, and smoke for 3 to 4 hours or until the internal temperature in the breast or thigh reads 160°F, or the juices run clear.

Chicken with Champagne Sauce

SMOKED CHICKEN AND RICE SALAD

Serves 4

Four 5-oz boneless, skinless chicken breasts

Nonstick cooking spray
2 Tbsp lemon pepper
1 Tbsp garlic salt
⅔ cup wild rice
⅔ cup brown rice
⅔ cup water

FOR THE SALAD DRESSING

⅔ cup bottled Italian salad dressing
½ cup mayonnaise
1 Tbsp hot sauce
2 tsp Worcestershire sauce
1 tsp sea salt
1 tsp fresh ground black pepper
½ cup pecans, toasted and chopped
6 scallions, chopped
½ tsp paprika

Spray the chicken breast all over with the cooking spray. Combine the lemon pepper and garlic salt in a bowl and blend well. Season the chicken with the mixture. Place in a stovetop smoker with wood chips of your choice and smoke until done, 30 to 40 minutes. Remove from the smoker and set aside on a plate.

Place the water in a saucepan with a tight-fitting lid. Combine the rice and water and bring to a boil, stirring. Reduce the heat, cover, and simmer until the rice is done.

In a medium bowl combine the Italian dressing, mayonnaise, hot sauce, Worcestershire sauce, salt, and pepper and blend with a wire whisk. Cover and set aside.

This salad can be served hot or chilled. Dice or cut the chicken breasts into chunks or strips, mix with the wild rice mixture, and toss. Add the nuts and scallions, top with dressing, sprinkle with paprika, mix gently and serve.

Tea-smoked Duck with Fragrant Rice

Serves 2 to 4

3 Tbsp kosher salt
1 Tbsp Szechuan peppercorns
One 5-lb duckling, dressed and
   rinsed
6 scallions, trimmed
1 Tbsp grated gingerroot
³/₄ cup white rice
¹/₂ cup black tea leaves
¹/₄ cup cane sugar

Add the salt and peppercorns to a dry heavy skillet and heat over a moderate heat until the peppercorns are fragrant. Allow to cool then place in a dish towel and crush with a rolling pin or a wood mallet.

Flatten the duck slightly by pressing down on the breastbone to break it. Rub the duck inside and out with the salt and peppercorn mixture. Place the duck in a large roasting pan, invert a plate on top, and weight the duck down with a heavy brick or weight covered with plastic wrap. Marinate for 1 to 2 days.

Rinse the duck. Put the scallions and ginger in the cavity. Steam or boil the duck until tender, 1 to 1¹/₂ hours. (Boiling is faster, but steaming produces a better result.) Remove the duck and drain.

Line a roasting pan or wok with foil. Combine the rice, tea leaves, and sugar in a small bowl and pour over the foil. Place the duck on a rack over the tea mixture and seal the pan as tightly as possible. If you cover the pan with plastic wrap and then foil you get a better seal.

Set the pan over high heat for 5 minutes. Reduce the heat to medium and heat for 15 to 20 minutes. Remove from the heat and allow to rest, uncovered, for 30 minutes. Allow to cool. Chop the duck into 1- to 2-inch pieces, bones and all, and cut the meat into strips. Serve at room temperature with the fragrant rice and your favorite barbecue or dipping sauce to the side.

Fragrant rice

Serves 6 to 8

1 cup white rice
¹/₄ cup peanut oil
2 Tbsp grated gingerroot
1 Tbsp garlic, minced
¹/₄ cup diced pimento
6 scallions, chopped
3 Tbsp soy sauce
1 Tbsp cane sugar
1 tsp sea salt
2 cups water

Heat the oil in a saucepan that has a tight-fitting lid. Add the rice and brown, stirring constantly, taking care not to burn. Add the ginger and garlic and sauté for a further minute. Add the pimento and onion, sauté for a further 30 seconds, stir in the soy sauce, sugar, and salt and cook for a further minute. Add the water and bring to a boil. Reduce the heat and cook until the rice is soft and tender.

SMOKED CHICKEN BREAST SANDWICH
WITH BASIL OLIVE PESTO

Serves 8

FOR THE MARINADE

¼ cup fresh lemon juice
¼ cup balsamic vinegar
4 cloves garlic, minced
1 tsp dried oregano
1 tsp lemon pepper
1 tsp salt
¼ cup virgin olive oil

Eight 5-oz boneless, skinless
  chicken breasts
2 cups boiling water
3 to 4 oz sun-dried tomatoes, not
  packed in oil
One 20-in loaf Italian bread
½ cup basil olive pesto
½ head arugula, washed and dried

Combine the lemon juice, vinegar, garlic, oregano, lemon pepper, and salt in a bowl and beat in the oil with a wire whisk until well blended. Place the chicken breasts in a zip-lock type plastic bag or a nonreactive baking pan. Pour the marinade over the chicken, cover, and marinate for 2 to 4 hours in the refrigerator.

Remove the chicken breasts from the marinade and place on the rack in the pan smoker. Add wood chips and heat until the chips start to smoke. Cover with the lid and smoke for about 30 minutes or until done.

In a heatproof bowl pour the boiling water over the tomatoes, cover, and allow to stand for 20 to 30 minutes or until soft. Drain the tomatoes and pat dry.

Cut the loaf of bread in half horizontally and spread with basil olive pesto. Slice the chicken breasts and place on the bottom half of the loaf, top with tomatoes and arugula, cover with the top of the loaf, and secure with cocktail sticks.

Basil olive pesto

Yield about ¾ cup

2 cloves garlic, chopped
1 cup fresh basil leaves, rinsed and
  patted dry
1 cup fresh flat-leaf parsley, minced
¼ cup pine nuts
¼ cup olive oil
¼ cup Kalamata or other brine-
  cured olives, pitted and
  chopped fine

Place the garlic in a running food processor. Add the basil, parsley, and nuts and blend well. Add the oil in a thin stream and blend until smooth. Transfer to a bowl and stir in the olives. Use at room temperature.

Lamb Sausages with Basque White Bean Stew and Mixed Green Salad

Makes 5 lb

3 lb ground lamb
2 lb ground pork or beef
2 Tbsp dried mint leaves
1 Tbsp granulated garlic
1 Tbsp seasoned salt
1 Tbsp crushed red peppers
2 tsp fine ground black pepper
2 tsp granulated onion
1 tsp dried savory
$\frac{1}{2}$ tsp mace

Combine the mint, garlic, salt, red pepper, black pepper, onion, savory, and mace in a small bowl and blend well.

Mix the ground lamb and pork together in a large bowl. Add the seasoning a third at a time and blend in thoroughly.

Form into sausage shapes. Place on smoker and smoke for 2 to 3 hours or until the internal temperature is 160°F, turning the sausages about halfway through the cooking process.

Basque white bean stew

Serves 8 to 10

2 cups dried Great Northern or
other white beans

1 large leek, cut in half lengthwise
and rinsed

1 green bell pepper, seeded and
halved

1 sweet red pepper, seeded and
halved

1/4 cup olive oil

2 cups diced onions

1 Tbsp paprika

1 tsp sea salt

1 tsp fresh ground black pepper

Rinse the beans in cold water. Place the beans in a large bowl and cover with 1 to 2 inches of cold water. Soak for at least 8 hours or overnight. Drain the beans and rinse again. Place in a large stockpot.

Add the leek and peppers to the pot and pour in enough cold water to cover the beans and vegetables by 2 to 3 inches. Bring to a boil and cook rapidly for 2 to 3 minutes, skimming the foam from the surface. Reduce the heat and simmer for about 2 hours. Add about 1/4 to 1/2 cup cold water every half hour. Simmer until the beans are tender.

In a heavy-bottomed skillet, heat the oil over medium heat. Add the onions and sauté until they are soft, about 8 to 10 minutes. Add the paprika and cook for a further 2 minutes. Add to the beans and season with the salt and pepper.

Discard the leek and peppers if desired, or chop up and return to the beans stirring to mix.

Mixed green salad with green goddess dressing

Serves 8 to 10

1 small head Romaine lettuce,
chopped or torn

2 heads Boston Bibb lettuce,
chopped or torn

1/4 cup mayonnaise

3 Tbsp minced chives

2 Tbsp plain yogurt

2 Tbsp Dijon mustard

1 Tbsp white wine vinegar

1 Tbsp fresh tarragon leaves,
minced

1 Tbsp fresh parsley, minced

1 tsp anchovy paste or to taste

1 tsp sea salt

1/2 tsp white pepper

1 bunch watercress, stems removed
and rinsed

1 red onion, diced

1 cucumber, peeled, seeded, and
diced

1 cup cherry tomatoes, rinsed and
halved

Rinse the lettuces and pat dry with a dish towel. Combine the mayonnaise, chives, yogurt, mustard, vinegar, tarragon, parsley, anchovy paste, salt, and pepper in a bowl and blend well with a wire whisk.

In a large bowl combine the watercress, Romaine, Bibb lettuce, onion, cucumber, and cherry tomatoes and blend well. Serve the salad and either spoon the dressing over or serve on the side.

WOOD-ROASTED SWEET RED PEPPERS

Serves 4 to 6

3 medium sweet red peppers
One 1-in piece grapevine cutting
5 cloves garlic, thin sliced
$\frac{1}{4}$ cup extra-virgin olive oil
1 Tbsp boiling water
2 tsp paprika
1 tsp cane sugar
$\frac{1}{2}$ tsp sea salt

Roast the peppers directly over a gas flame, under a broiler, or over a hot charcoal and wood fire, turning frequently until charred all over. Place the peppers in a paper bag and seal. Set aside for 10 minutes to steam. Scrape off the blackened skin and remove the cores, seeds, and ribs. Rinse the peppers and pat dry with paper towels.

Place the grapevine cutting in the bottom of your stovetop smoker; place the rack over the cutting. Heat until the grapevine starts smoking, about 3 minutes. Place the peppers on the rack, cover, and smoke for 5 minutes. Remove the peppers, place on a plate or tray, and allow to cool slightly. Slice into $\frac{1}{2}$-in wide slices.

In a heavy skillet, cook the garlic in the olive oil over a medium heat until slightly soft, about 2 minutes. Add the pepper strips, reduce the heat to low, and cook for 10 to 15 minutes, stirring occasionally. In a small bowl combine the paprika, sugar, salt, and water and set aside. When the peppers are ready, add the paprika water and cook for a further 5 to 10 minutes. Serve warm or at room temperature, drizzled with a little olive oil, or use to top foccacia bread.

RATATOUILLE PACKAGES

Serves 6 to 8

1 medium eggplant, peeled and
    cubed
1 large red onion, peeled and cut
    into 1½-in pieces
1 large red bell pepper, seeded and
    cut into 1½-in pieces
1 large yellow bell pepper, seeded
    and cut into 1½-in pieces
1 medium zucchini, quartered and
    cut into 1-in pieces
4 large cloves garlic, minced
¼ cup olive oil
2 cups Roma tomatoes, peeled,
    seeded, and cut into bite-size
    pieces
3 Tbsp fresh basil leaves, minced
3 Tbsp fresh lemon juice
2 Tbsp capers
2 Tbsp fresh flat-leaf parsley,
    minced
2 Tbsp fresh curly parsley, minced
1 tsp sea salt
1 tsp fresh ground black pepper

Combine the eggplant, onion, red bell pepper, yellow bell pepper, zucchini, and garlic in a large bowl. Pour the olive oil over the vegetables and toss to coat. Place in a 9 x 13-in baking pan and cover with plastic wrap, then with foil to seal. Place on your cooker and cook for about 1 hour. Combine the tomatoes, basil, lemon juice, capers, both types of parsley, salt, and pepper and toss to mix. Remove the pan from the cooker and take off the foil and plastic wrap. Add the tomato mixture and blend together. Place back in your cooker and add wood chips or other smoking material to your fire and smoke, stirring occasionally, for a further hour or until done to your liking.

TERIYAKI ONIONS

Serves 6 to 8

FOR THE TERIYAKI SAUCE

2 cups pineapple juice
1½ cups soy sauce
1 cup cane sugar
1 Tbsp grated gingerroot
2 cloves garlic, minced
1 Tbsp arrowroot or
    2¼ tsp cornstarch
2 Tbsp cold water

6 to 8 small or medium onions

First make the sauce. Place the pineapple juice, soy sauce, sugar, ginger, and garlic in a saucepan and bring to a boil over medium heat, stirring to dissolve and incorporate the sugar. Take care not to let the mixture boil over. Combine the arrowroot and cold water in a small bowl and make a paste. Add to the boiling mixture, stirring with a wire whisk. Bring back to a boil. Reduce the heat and simmer until a sheen forms, about 2 minutes. Remove from the heat and set aside.

Peel the onions and using a sharp, thin knife cut down to the root core, but not through it. Repeat this cut at least 7 more times. Place each onion in the center of a foil sheet and bring the sides of the foil up around the onion. Pour ¼ cup teriyaki sauce over each onion and twist the foil to seal. Place the foil packages on your cooker and cook for at least 1½ hours, longer if desired. The timing is not critical because if the onions are sweet you can eat them raw, cold, or hot. Remove the onions from their foil packages and they will look like open flowers. Serve the remainder of the sauce on the side or top with a tablespoon of sauce.

POTATO, PEA, AND MUSHROOM PACKAGES

Serves 8

4 large russet potatoes, washed and
    dried
1 stick butter, sliced into 8 even
    pieces, more if desired
2 cups frozen peas, defrosted
2 cups fresh mushrooms, sliced
2 tsp sea salt
1 tsp fresh ground black pepper

Cut the potatoes in half lengthwise. Slice each half into about $^1/_8$-inch slices and place in the center of a 12 x 12-inch piece of foil. Top the potatoes with a piece of butter, $^1/_4$ cup peas, and mushroom slices. Combine the salt and pepper together in a bowl and blend well. Season the potatoes to taste with the salt and pepper mixture. Seal the foil packages, place on your cooker, and cook for 1 to 2 hours or until the potatoes are done.

SMOKED EGGPLANT PACKAGE

Serves 6 to 8

$^1/_4$ cup extra-virgin olive oil
2 Tbsp fresh lemon juice
4 large cloves garlic, minced
1 tsp sea salt
$^1/_2$ tsp fresh ground black pepper
1 large eggplant, about 1$^1/_2$ lb,
    cut into $^1/_2$-in slices
$^1/_2$ tsp dried thyme

Combine the olive oil, lemon juice, garlic, salt, and pepper in a small bowl and blend well. Dip the sliced eggplant into the mixture and place in the center of a large piece of foil. Pour the remaining marinade over the slices and season with the thyme. Seal the foil package, folding over several times to ensure it is airtight. Place on your cooker and cook for about 1 hour. Carefully open the foil package and roll down the sides to form a pan. If there is too much liquid in the package, drain some of it off. Add smoking wood chips and smoke for a further $^1/_2$ to 1 hour to obtain the smoke flavor you desire.

WHISKEY-MUSTARD GLAZED HAM

Serves 12 to 15

One 15-lb precooked smoked
    bone-in ham
Whole cloves

FOR THE GLAZE

1 cup Dijon mustard
2 cups dark brown sugar
$^1/_3$ cup whiskey
1 tsp sea salt
1 tsp fresh ground black pepper

Trim the skin and excess fat from the ham. With a sharp knife score the ham fat in 1-inch squares. Place a whole clove in the center of each square. If you have trouble inserting the clove into the ham, pierce the hole with a skewer or cocktail stick.

Place the ham in your cooker and smoke for 5 to 8 hours, longer if desired. After the ham has been in the cooker at least 4 hours, combine the mustard, brown sugar, whiskey, salt, and pepper in a bowl with a heavy spoon or wire whisk. Brush this glaze over the ham with a pastry brush or, if preferred, spoon it on.

PAN-SMOKED SALMON WITH ASPARAGUS AND MUSHROOMS

Serves 4 to 6

1 cup mayonnaise
2 Tbsp balsamic vinegar
One 3-lb salmon fillet, with pin
  bones removed
1 Tbsp bay seasoning (see page 26)
2 Tbsp fresh dill
3 Tbsp toasted sesame oil
2 tsp grated gingerroot
2 large cloves garlic, minced
2 shallots, sliced thin
8 oz chestnut or small oyster
  mushrooms, stems removed
2 Tbsp fish sauce
1 Tbsp soy sauce
1 tsp cane sugar
1½ to 2 lb fresh asparagus
2 tsp olive oil

In a small bowl combine the mayonnaise and balsamic vinegar, blending well. Season the salmon with the bay seasoning, top with the mayonnaise mixture and top that with the dill. Place hickory wood chips or any other wood chips of your choice in the smoker. Place the rack in the bottom and heat until the chips start to smoke, then place the fish on the rack, cover, and smoke 20 to 40 minutes or until the fish flakes easily.

Heat the sesame oil in a skillet over medium heat and sauté ginger, garlic, and shallots for about 2 minutes, stirring constantly. Add the mushrooms, fish sauce, soy sauce, and sugar and cook, stirring occasionally, until the mushrooms are soft. Set aside and keep warm.

Trim the asparagus and cut the tough stalks. Lightly brush or spray a grill pan with oil then place on moderate heat until hot. Add the asparagus and cook, turning occasionally for 10 minutes or until they begin to char.

To serve, carefully divide the salmon into 4 to 6 portions. Divide the asparagus and top with the mushroom mixture. Serve warm.

Scallop and Shrimp Brochettes
with Curried Rice Pilaf

Serves 6 to 8

1 to 2 lb scallops, shucked and rinsed
1 to 2 lb shrimp, peeled and deveined
2 sticks butter, melted
2 Tbsp fresh lemon juice
2 tsp fresh ground black pepper
1 tsp paprika
1 lemon, cut into wedges

FOR THE MARINADE

1 cup dry white wine
2 Tbsp balsamic vinegar
2 Tbsp fresh lemon juice
¼ cup sunflower oil
1 Tbsp fresh tarragon leaves, minced
1 tsp fresh basil leaves, minced
1 tsp fresh thyme leaves, minced
1 tsp fresh oregano leaves, minced
1 tsp cane sugar
1 tsp sea salt
1 tsp fresh ground black pepper

For the marinade combine the wine, vinegar, lemon juice, oil, tarragon, basil, thyme, oregano, sugar, salt, and pepper in a nonreactive bowl and blend well with a wire whisk. Place the scallops and shrimp in the marinade, tossing to coat evenly. Cover and marinate for 2 to 4 hours in the refrigerator.

Drain the marinated scallops and shrimp and thread them onto long metal skewers, threading the scallops through their diameter. Combine the melted butter and lemon juice. Brush the scallops and shrimp with the butter mixture and season with pepper and paprika. Place on your cooker and smoke for 30 minutes to 1 hour or until done, basting with the butter-lemon mixture every 15 minutes. Serve with lemon wedges.

Curried rice pilaf

Serves 6 to 8

2 Tbsp olive oil
2 Tbsp butter
3 cloves garlic, minced
1½ cups converted rice
2 chicken bouillon cubes
½ cup diced red onions

½ cup diced celery
¼ cup diced pimentos
1 Tbsp curry powder
1 tsp black pepper
3 cups water
6 scallions, sliced thin

Heat the olive oil and butter over medium heat and sauté the garlic, stirring constantly. Add the rice and crumble in the chicken bouillon cubes. Sauté until golden brown, stirring frequently so the rice does not scorch. Add the onions, celery, pimentos, curry powder, and pepper and cook, stirring, for 2 minutes. Pour in the water and bring to a boil. Add the scallions, cover, and simmer for 5 minutes. Remove from the heat and allow to stand for 30 minutes. Serve warm.

SPICED ROCK CORNISH HENS
WITH CITRUS ORZO

Serves 8 to 10

2 Tbsp toasted cumin seeds
One 3-in cinnamon stick, broken
   into pieces
8 whole cloves
¼ cup paprika
2 tsp cane sugar
1 tsp cayenne
1 tsp sea salt
4 large cloves garlic, minced
1 tsp sea salt
1 Tbsp fresh lemon zest
Juice of 1 lemon
¼ cup olive oil
Eight 12-oz rock Cornish hens or
   2 whole 3-lb chickens
½ stick sweet butter
2 Tbsp fresh parsley, minced

FOR THE SAUCE

2 cups Melba sauce (raspberry
   sauce)
2 Tbsp butter
1 to 2 oz Grand Marnier
2 Tbsp cold water (optional)
1 Tbsp cornstarch (optional)

Put the cumin seeds, cinnamon, and cloves in a spice grinder or mortar and pestle and pulverize. Combine the ground spices with the paprika, sugar, cayenne, and salt, blending well. Work the garlic and salt to a paste. Combine the garlic paste, zest, lemon juice, oil, and two tablespoons of the spice mixture (reserve the remainder) in a nonreactive bowl and blend well.

If you are using whole chickens, cut into quarters. Rub rock Cornish hens or chicken pieces all over with the garlic marinade. Place in a glass baking pan, cover, and allow to marinate for at least 2 hours, but no longer than 4 hours, in the refrigerator.

To cook, place on your smoker, skin-side up or breast-up if using rock Cornish hens and season with the reserved spice mixture. Melt the butter in a small saucepan and combine with the parsley. Cook for two hours, basting with the butter mixture every 20 minutes for the last hour. Rock Cornish hens are done when they reach an internal temperature of 160°F or when the juices run clear. To make the sauce, combine the Melba sauce, butter, and Grand Marnier in a saucepan and bring to a fast simmer. Do not boil. If you want a thicker sauce combine the cornstarch and cold water and blend in with a wire whisk until thick and glossy. Serve the rock Cornish hens with citrus orzo and sauce on the side.

Citrus orzo

1 lb orzo
7 cups chicken broth
1 Tbsp olive oil
¼ cup fresh lemon juice
¼ cup fresh basil leaves, minced
¼ cup fresh parsley, minced
¼ cup fresh mint leaves, minced
1 Tbsp lemon zest
1 tsp sea salt
1 tsp fresh ground black pepper

Bring the chicken stock to a boil in a large saucepan. Add the orzo and cook, stirring often to prevent sticking, until most of the broth is absorbed and the orzo is tender and creamy, about 10 minutes. Remove from the heat and stir in the oil, lemon juice, basil, parsley, mint, and lemon zest. Season with the salt and pepper. Serve warm.

Halibut with Bread Crumbs and Smoke-roasted Tomato Sauce

Serves 4

1 cup fresh white bread crumbs
2 Tbsp fresh tarragon leaves, minced

FOR THE SAUCE

$\frac{1}{4}$ to $\frac{1}{2}$ cup extra-virgin olive oil
1 lb plum tomatoes, halved and seeded
1 head garlic
$\frac{1}{4}$ cup balsamic vinegar
2 tsp cane sugar
1 tsp sea salt
1 tsp fresh ground black pepper
$\frac{1}{4}$ cup water (optional)
$\frac{1}{4}$ cup mayonnaise
2 tsp Dijon mustard
Four 6- to 8-oz fresh halibut fillets
2 Tbsp sea salt
1 Tbsp fresh ground black pepper
1 Tbsp fresh tarragon leaves

In a small bowl combine the bread crumbs and tarragon and blend well. Cover and set aside.

Place the olive oil in a large bowl. Add the tomatoes and garlic, tossing to coat evenly. Place the tomatoes and garlic on the rack of a smoke pan. Add $\frac{1}{4}$ cup hickory sawdust or chips and heat over high heat until the chips start to smoke, about 3 minutes. Cover, reduce the heat, and smoke for about 20 to 30 minutes or until the tomatoes are lightly browned and the garlic is tender when pierced with a knife. (The garlic may take a little longer, 10 to 15 minutes.) Peel the garlic and place in a blender fitted with a steel blade, add the tomatoes, vinegar, sugar, salt, and pepper and purée until smooth. Add some water if the sauce seems too thick. Place in a saucepan and warm. Set aside and keep warm.

Combine the mayonnaise and mustard in a small bowl. Season the fillets all over with salt and pepper. Spread the mayonnaise mixture over the top of the fillets and pat the seasoned bread crumbs evenly on top. Place in your smoker pan and smoke with wood chips of your choice for 10 to 15 minutes or until the fish flakes easily. Serve with fresh tarragon sprinkled over.

SMOKE-ROASTING RECIPES

SMOKE-ROASTING is by far is my favorite method. There are several rules that will make your smoke roasting a success. The first one is to have fun and enjoy yourself! The second is to keep records of quantities and cooking times for future reference, and finally, it is important to maintain as constant a temperature as possible during cooking.

For those unfamiliar with smoking, these recipes have been written to ensure that you succeed the very first time you try them. You will gain great satisfaction from knowing that this great food has been produced by your very own hands, which have learnt to apply spices and seasonings, and to control the temperatures and level of smoke.

Pork Tenderloin Havana

with Black Bean Sauce and Fried Plantains

Serves 8 to 10

FOR THE MARINADE

3 oranges
4 limes
1 cup olive oil
1 Tbsp grated orange zest
1 Tbsp grated lime zest
2 tsp crushed red peppers
1 tsp kosher salt
$\frac{1}{2}$ cup fresh cilantro, minced
2 bay leaves, crushed
$\frac{1}{4}$ cup sherry vinegar
Lime or sour orange wedges, sour
    cream, and sliced red onions

Four 1-lb pork tenderloins, trimmed
    of membrane and fat

Roll the oranges and limes on your counter top, this will release more juice from them. Cut and squeeze the oranges and limes into a large nonreactive bowl, then peel and chop the fruit. Add the fruit, olive oil, zest, crushed red peppers, salt, cilantro, and bay leaves and mix well. Place the pork in a glass baking pan or self-locking plastic bag and pour the marinade over, making sure that the meat is evenly coated. Cover or seal and marinate for 8 hours or overnight in the refrigerator.

Remove the meat from the marinade and place on your cooker. Smoke for 2 to 3 hours or until it reaches a temperature of 145 to 160°F. To serve, slice into $\frac{1}{2}$-inch slices, top with bean sauce and sprinkle over the sherry vinegar. Serve with the fried plantains and garnish with lime or sour orange wedges, sour cream, and red onion slices.

Black bean sauce

Serves 8 to 10

$\frac{1}{4}$ lb bacon, diced
$\frac{1}{4}$ cup peanut oil
1 cup diced red onions
1 medium jalapeño chile, diced
2 stalks celery, diced
2 cups black turtle beans, soaked in water overnight
3 Tbsp toasted ground cumin
1 tsp cayenne
1 bay leaf
1 tsp black pepper
8 cups chicken broth
1 to 2 Tbsp sea salt

In a large saucepot sauté the bacon squares in the peanut oil until almost done. Add the onions, jalapeño, and celery and cook until soft. Drain the beans and cook for 2 minutes, stirring. Add the cumin, cayenne, bay leaf, and pepper and stir. Add the broth and bring to a boil. Cook the beans until soft. Adjust the seasoning if necessary. Set aside and keep warm.

Fried plantains

Serves 8 to 10

1 to 2 plantains, peeled and cut on an extreme
    bias into $\frac{1}{2}$-in slices
1 cup all-purpose flour
1 tsp ground cinnamon
1 tsp fresh ground black pepper
1 tsp sea salt
$\frac{1}{4}$ cup clarified butter

Dredge the plantains in the flour, seasoned with cinnamon, pepper, and salt. Gently sauté the plantains in the clarified butter until golden brown. Drain on paper towels until ready to serve. If necessary sauté the plantains again to crisp them up before serving.

CHINESE BARBECUED PORK

Serves 6 to 8

FOR THE MARINADE

1 cup soy sauce
¼ cup hoisin sauce
¼ cup light brown sugar, packed
2 Tbsp liquid honey
2 Tbsp sherry
2 tsp grated gingerroot
1 large clove garlic, minced
1 Tbsp red food coloring (optional)
1 tsp ground cinnamon
½ tsp Chinese five-spice powder
Scallion curls to garnish

Four 1-lb pork tenderloins, trimmed
**   of membrane and fat**

Combine the soy sauce, hoisin sauce, sugar, honey, sherry, ginger, garlic, food coloring, cinnamon, and five-spice powder in a bowl and blend well. Place the tenderloins in a nonreactive dish or plastic bag and pour the marinade over them. Marinate for 2 to 4 hours in the refrigerator, turning occasionally. Remove the tenderloins from the marinade, reserving the marinade, and place on your cooker. Smoke until the internal temperature reaches 145 to 165°F. Do not overcook. Baste with the reserved marinade every 30 minutes. Serve hot or cold, cut on a diagonal on a bed of scallion curls, as an entrée, appetizer, Chinese salad, or sandwich filling.

Use hoisin and chile sauce for dipping, if you like.

GUAVA-GLAZED BABY BACK RIBS

Serves 8 to 10

FOR THE ISLAND DRY RUB

¼ cup brown sugar
¼ cup cane sugar
2 Tbsp seasoned salt
2 Tbsp garlic salt
2 Tbsp celery salt
2 Tbsp chili powder
2 Tbsp fine ground black pepper
1 tsp ground allspice
1 tsp ground ginger
½ tsp cayenne
¼ tsp ground cloves
⅛ tsp mace

FOR THE GLAZE

1 cup guava paste or fruit purée such as
  mango or plum
¼ cup light honey
¼ cup orange juice
2 Tbsp soy sauce
2 Tbsp fresh lime juice
1 tsp ground ginger
½ tsp ground allspice
1 tsp sea salt
½ tsp white pepper

4 racks baby back pork ribs (1 to 2 lb each)

Make the rub. Combine the brown sugar, cane sugar, seasoned salt, garlic salt, celery salt, chili powder, pepper, allspice, ginger, cayenne, cloves, and mace in a bowl and blend well. Place in an airtight container. Set aside until ready to use.

For the glaze, combine the guava paste, honey, orange juice, soy sauce, lime juice, ginger, allspice, salt, and pepper in a saucepan and heat over a medium-low heat, stirring with a wire whisk. Heat for about 10 minutes until the sauce is well incorporated. Set aside and keep warm.

Remove the membrane from the back of the ribs. Sprinkle both sides of each rack of ribs with the rub. Place on your pit and cook indirectly for 4 to 6 hours, turning after 2 hours then again 1 hour later. To test if the ribs are done take two ribs side by side and see if they tear apart easily. If they are about done coat each slab on both sides with the glaze, using a pastry brush, then cook for 10 to 15 minutes and repeat the process. Remove the ribs from your cooker, allowing the ribs to rest for 10 to 15 minutes. Cut into serving pieces as desired. Enjoy and take all of the credit—you deserve it!

JAMAICAN JERKED PORK TENDERLOIN

Serves 6 to 8

FOR THE WET JERK RUB

3 cups packed scallions,
   cut into 1-in pieces
1/4 cup fresh thyme leaves
3 Tbsp grated gingerroot
2 Tbsp fresh lime juice
1 Tbsp ground coriander
1 Tbsp ground black pepper
5 large cloves garlic, minced
2 Scotch Bonnet chiles, seeded
   and halved
2 tsp sea salt
2 tsp ground allspice
1 tsp ground nutmeg
1 tsp ground cinnamon
1/2 tsp powdered bay leaf
3 Tbsp peanut oil

Four 1-lb pork tenderloins, trimmed
   of membrane and fat

Because this rub contains chiles, wear rubber gloves while preparing it. Combine the onions, thyme, gingerroot, lime juice, coriander, pepper, garlic, Scotch Bonnet chiles, salt, allspice, nutmeg, cinnamon, and bay leaf in a blender fitted with a steel blade and process until smooth. Add the oil in a thin stream while processing, until it is all incorporated.

Divide the jerk mixture in half. Place the tenderloins in a glass baking pan and, wearing rubber gloves, rub all over with the mixture. Cover and marinate for 4 hours in the refrigerator. Remove from the marinade and smoke-roast for about 2 hours or until the internal temperature reaches 145 to 160°F. Baste with the reserved marinade every 30 minutes. This dish is good served with rice and beans, and chile sauce.

GLAZED VEAL RIBLETS

Serves 6 to 8

FOR THE MARINADE AND
GLAZE

1 cup fresh lemon juice
1 cup clover honey
1/2 cup scallions, sliced thin
1/4 cup hoisin sauce
1/4 cup sesame oil
1/4 cup pineapple juice
2 Tbsp grated gingerroot
2 Tbsp minced garlic
1 Tbsp grated lemon zest
1 tsp sea salt

6 pounds veal riblets, 2 1/2 in long,
   cut into 2-rib sections and
   trimmed

Combine the lemon juice, honey, scallions, hoisin sauce, sesame oil, pineapple juice, gingerroot, garlic, lemon zest, and salt in a bowl and blend well with a wire whisk to emulsify. Pour the marinade over the riblets, turning to coat well. Cover and marinate for 4 to 6 hours in the refrigerator. Remove the veal from the marinade, reserving it to use as a glaze. Place on your cooker and cook for 4 to 5 hours or until the ribs tear easily, brushing with the glaze 15 minutes before they are ready.

Jamaican Jerked Pork Tenderloin

Memphis-style Pork Loin
with Barbecue sauce

Serves 8 to 10

FOR THE MEMPHIS
BARBECUE RUB

2 Tbsp sea salt
1 Tbsp light brown cane sugar
1 tsp lemon pepper
1 tsp fine ground black pepper
1 tsp cayenne
1 tsp chili powder
1 tsp dry mustard
1 tsp garlic powder
1/2 tsp ground cinnamon

**One 3- to 4-lb boneless pork loin,
   trimmed**
1/2 cup yellow mustard

FOR THE MEMPHIS
BASTING SAUCE

1 cup cider or red wine vinegar
1 cup water or broth

To make the rub combine the salt, sugar, lemon pepper, pepper, cayenne, chili powder, dry mustard, garlic, and cinnamon in a bowl and blend well. Store in an airtight container in a cool dark place.

Rub or paint the pork loin all over with the yellow mustard using a pastry brush. Season all over with the rub. Place on your cooker and smoke for 3 to 5 hours or until the internal temperature is 145 to 160°F. Combine the ingredients for the basting sauce and use to baste the pork after 1 1/2 hours; baste every 30 to 45 minutes. If preferred, apple juice or cider can replace the basting sauce. During the last 30 to 45 minutes, glaze, using 1 cup of the barbecue sauce.

Barbecue sauce

2 cups catsup
1 cup cider vinegar
1 stick butter
1/2 cup dark brown cane sugar
1/4 cup yellow mustard
1/4 cup Worcestershire sauce
1 tsp Tabasco sauce
3 whole lemons

To make the barbecue sauce combine the catsup, vinegar, butter, sugar, mustard, Worcestershire sauce, Tabasco sauce, and lemons in a saucepan over medium heat. Squeeze the juice out of the lemons into the sauce through a sieve, to remove the seeds and add the pulp and zest to the mixture. Bring to a boil, stirring with a wire whisk. Reduce the heat and simmer for 30 minutes. Remove the lemons before serving.

ROSEMARY AND GARLIC PORK ROAST
WITH BALSAMIC RHUBARB COMPOTE

Serves 4 to 6

FOR THE DIJON MUSTARD
SLATHER

¼ cup Dijon mustard
2 Tbsp flat beer
2 tsp brown sugar
½ tsp hot sauce
½ tsp salt
½ tsp fresh ground black pepper

One 4½ to 5-lb 8 bone-in pork rib
  roast, trimmed
4 large cloves garlic, sliced thin
2 Tbsp fresh rosemary leaves

Combine the mustard, beer, brown sugar, hot sauce, salt, and pepper and blend well. Cover and set aside. With a sharp-pointed paring knife cut slits about 1 inch apart in the fat of the meat and insert a sliver of garlic in the cuts. With a pastry brush, paint the roast with the mustard slather and sprinkle it with the rosemary leaves.

Place the roast in your smoker and smoke for about 3 hours at 230 to 250°F or until the internal temperature is 145 to 160°F. Allow to rest for about 15 minutes, slice, and serve with balsamic rhubarb compote.

Balsamic rhubarb compote

1 cup cane sugar
¼ cup balsamic vinegar
1 tsp grated gingerroot
½ tsp sea salt
2 cups diced fresh rhubarb stalks

Combine the sugar, vinegar, gingerroot, and salt in a saucepan and bring to a boil, stirring to dissolve the sugar and salt. Stir in the rhubarb and simmer until tender but still crisp, 1 to 2 minutes. Transfer the rhubarb with a slotted spoon to a bowl. Simmer the sugar water until it has thickened. Remove from the heat and stir in the rhubarb. Serve the compote warm or at room temperature.

LIME AND GARLIC PORK TENDERLOIN
WITH JALAPEÑO ONION MARMALADE

Serves 4

FOR THE MARINADE

¼ cup fresh lime juice
4 cloves garlic, chopped
2 Tbsp soy sauce
2 Tbsp grated gingerroot
1 Tbsp Dijon mustard
1 tsp sea salt
½ tsp fresh ground black pepper
½ tsp cayenne
½ cup olive oil

Four ¾-lb pork tenderloins, trimmed

Combine the lime juice, garlic, soy sauce, gingerroot, mustard, salt, pepper, cayenne, and oil in a blender or food processor fitted with a steel blade. Process until well blended, about 1 to 2 minutes.

Place the tenderloins in a glass baking pan or in a zip-lock type plastic bag; pour the marinade over the tenderloins and cover or seal. Marinate for 4 to 5 hours in the refrigerator or overnight.

Remove the pork from the marinade, reserving the marinade, and place on your smoker. Smoke for 1½ to 2 hours or until the internal temperature reaches 145 to 160°F. Allow to rest for 10 to 15 minutes, slice, and serve warm with jalapeño onion marmalade and a salad of your choice.

Jalapeño onion marmalade

3 cups diced red onions
3 Tbsp sunflower oil
1 tsp sea salt
1 tsp fresh ground black pepper
2 fresh red jalapeño chiles, seeded and minced
2 Tbsp cane sugar
¼ cup red wine vinegar
¼ cup water

In a large skillet sauté the onions in the oil, with salt and pepper, over medium heat until soft, stirring occasionally. Add jalapeño chiles and cook for 1 minute, stirring. Add the sugar, stirring until dissolved. Add the vinegar and simmer, stirring until almost all the liquid is evaporated. Add the water and simmer, stirring until mixture is slightly thickened and the onions are very tender, about 8 to 10 minutes. Serve hot or at room temperature.

Pork Tenderloin with Cajun Crab, Shrimp, and Cheddar Cheese Stuffing

Serves 6 to 8

2 pork tenderloins (2- to 4-lb), trimmed of membrane and fat

FOR THE STUFFING

1 tsp sea salt
1 tsp white pepper
½ tsp fine ground black pepper
½ tsp cayenne
¼ tsp fresh thyme leaves
¼ tsp fresh oregano leaves
1 stick butter
1 cup minced onions
½ cup minced celery
4 large cloves garlic, minced
½ cup minced sweet red pepper
6 scallions, sliced very thin
½ lb fresh, frozen, or canned crab meat, picked over
½ lb fresh shrimp, peeled, deveined, and minced
¼ cup dry vermouth
2 cups very fine dried bread crumbs
½ stick sweet butter
1 large egg
½ cup shredded Cheddar cheese or grated Parmesan cheese

FOR THE LEMON BUTTER BASTE

1 stick butter, melted
2 Tbsp fresh lemon juice

Flatten the tenderloins by placing them between two pieces of waxed paper or plastic wrap and pounding them with a meat mallet. Cover and set aside in the refrigerator.

Combine the salt, white pepper, black pepper, cayenne, thyme, and oregano in a small bowl and blend well.

Place half the butter in a large nonstick skillet over medium-high heat, add the onions, celery, garlic, and red peppers and sauté until soft, about 4 to 5 minutes. Add the seasoning and blend well. Add the rest of the butter and scallions and sauté for about 3 minutes or until the butter is melted and hot. Add the crab and shrimp and sauté until just cooked, pour in the vermouth and sauté, stirring until the liquid has reduced by half. Stir in 1 cup bread crumbs and allow to cook, without stirring, until the mixture sticks, about 1 minute. Stir and scrape the bottom of the pan, then add the butter and continue cooking until the butter melts, stirring and scraping the pan bottom continuously. Stir in the remaining bread crumbs and remove from the heat; allow to cool slightly. Combine the egg with the cheese, add to the stuffing, and blend well. Transfer the stuffing to a shallow baking pan and refrigerate until well chilled.

Lay the flattened tenderloins on your work counter and divide the filling between the tenderloins. Spread out the stuffing to within 1 inch inside the meat and roll up like jelly-rolls. Place on your cooker and smoke for 2 to 3 hours or until the internal temperature is 160°F, basting with the lemon butter baste every 45 minutes as it cooks. To make the lemon butter baste, melt 1 stick butter with the lemon juice in a small saucepan over medium heat. When done allow to rest for about 10 to 15 minutes. Slice and serve warm, with your favorite barbecue sauce on the side.

Cajun Standing Roast with Sweet Pepper and Hot Chile Sauce

Serves 12 to 15

FOR THE CAJUN
SEASONING

1 Tbsp paprika
1 Tbsp cayenne
2 tsp dry mustard
2 tsp seasoned salt
1 tsp fine ground black pepper
1 tsp granulated garlic
1 tsp rubbed sage
½ tsp white pepper
½ tsp granulated onion
½ tsp ground cumin
½ tsp ground thyme
½ tsp ground oregano
½ tsp ground marjoram

**One 18-lb standing rib
(prime rib) roast**
**10 large cloves garlic, sliced
into slivers**

FOR THE SAUCE

¼ cup olive oil
4 cloves garlic, minced
**1 sweet red pepper, seeded, ribs
removed, and cut into thin strips**
**1 green bell pepper, seeded, ribs
removed, and cut into thin strips**
**1 yellow bell pepper, seeded, ribs
removed, and cut into thin strips**
**2 jalapeño chiles, seeded, ribs
removed, and cut into thin strips**
**2 Serrano chiles, seeded, ribs
removed, and cut into thin strips**
1 cup Marsala wine
1 quart rich brown sauce

Combine the paprika, cayenne, dry mustard, seasoned salt, black pepper, garlic, sage, white pepper, onion, cumin, thyme, oregano, and marjoram, blending well. Set aside.

Remove the fat and thick membrane from the back of the ribs. Using a sharp pointed knife, outline the bones with the knifepoint, penetrating about 1 inch. Pull back the flap that covers the meat but leave it attached.

Using a thin sharp knife, puncture the meat all over, making about 40 slits, and insert a sliver of garlic into each. Rub the Cajun seasoning all over the meat. Replace the flap, place in your cooker, and smoke for 4 to 6 hours or to an internal temperature of 130°F for medium-rare, or longer if desired.

While the meat is cooking, make the sauce. Heat the oil in a heavy saucepan and sauté the garlic, and chiles. Cook until soft. Towel off any excess oil. Deglaze the pan with the Marsala, and, over medium-low heat, carefully ignite to burn off the alcohol. Reduce the wine to a glaze. Add the brown sauce. Cook the sauce until reduced to a consistency that will coat the back of a spoon. Strain the sauce into a container and chill until ready to serve. Remove the roast and allow to stand for 30 minutes. Serve sliced with the sauce.

Remove any fat that forms on top of the sauce. Serve hot, spooned over the meat.

FESTIVE HAM WITH FRUIT AND NUT STUFFING

Serves 8 to 10

**Half a fresh ham, 5 to 6 lb, boned
and flattened**

FOR THE MARINADE

2 cups dry white wine
2 cups apple juice
$\frac{1}{2}$ cup cider vinegar
$\frac{1}{2}$ cup Calvados brandy
$\frac{1}{2}$ cup minced onions
$\frac{1}{4}$ cup brown sugar
1 Tbsp grated gingerroot
1 Tbsp whole allspice, crushed
1 Tbsp peppercorns, crushed
4 cloves garlic, minced
5 whole cloves
2 whole cinnamon sticks
$\frac{1}{2}$ tsp cardamom seeds, crushed

FOR THE STUFFING

$\frac{1}{2}$ stick sweet butter
2 bunches scallions, minced
4 large cloves garlic, minced
1 cup dried apricots
$\frac{1}{2}$ cup pistachio nuts, shelled
$\frac{1}{2}$ cup pine nuts, toasted
$\frac{1}{2}$ cup fresh parsley, minced
2 Tbsp grated lemon zest
1 Tbsp balsamic vinegar
1 Tbsp brown sugar
1 tsp fresh ground black pepper

Combine the wine, apple juice, vinegar, Calvados brandy, onions, gingerroot, sugar, allspice, peppercorns, garlic, cloves, cinnamon, and cardamom in a nonreactive bowl and blend well. Place the ham in a nonreactive baking pan or a zip-lock type plastic bag. Place in the refrigerator and marinate for 2 days, turning every 12 hours.

To make the stuffing melt the butter in a large skillet over medium-high heat. Add the scallions and garlic and sauté for 3 to 4 minutes. Remove from the heat and add the apricots, pistachio nuts, pine nuts, parsley, lemon zest, vinegar, sugar, and pepper, blending well. Place in a container, cover, and refrigerate for 2 days.

Remove the ham from the marinade and pat dry, using paper towels. Strain the marinade and set aside.

You can either stuff the ham or cook the stuffing separately. Spread the stuffing mixture over the inside of the ham to within 1 inch of the edges. Roll and tie together every 2 inches. If the skin is intact score it into a diamond pattern using a sharp knife. Place in the cooker and smoke until the internal temperature is 160°F, about 8 hours.

To cook the stuffing separately, place the mixture in a roasting pan and top it with the flattened ham; you may have to cut it in half. Place it skin-side up, inside the edges, cut a 1- x 1-inch diamond pattern. Place in the cooker and smoke until the internal temperature reaches 160°F. The cooking time will be 5 to 6 hours. Baste with the reserved marinade every hour.

CHILI-RUBBED RACK OF LAMB WITH PUMPKIN SEED SAUCE

Serves 2

¼ cup chili powder
1 Tbsp toasted ground cumin
1 Tbsp sugar
2 tsp granulated garlic
1 tsp dried oregano
1 tsp sea salt
1 tsp fresh ground black pepper
2 racks spring lamb, trimmed

FOR THE SAUCE

¼ cup fresh cilantro
¼ cup fresh mint leaves
¼ cup diced shallots
2 Tbsp raw pumpkin seeds
1 Serrano chile, chopped
2 Tbsp fresh lime juice
2 Tbsp water
2 Tbsp peanut oil
1 Tbsp sugar
1 tsp sea salt

Combine the chili powder, cumin, sugar, garlic, oregano, salt, and pepper in a bowl and blend well.

Season each rack of lamb with the chili seasoning and rub into the meat. Cover the racks and allow to rest for 1 hour at room temperature or overnight in the refrigerator.

Combine the cilantro, mint, shallots, pumpkin seeds, Serrano chile, lime juice, water, oil, sugar, and salt in a blender fitted with a steel blade. Purée until smooth, about 3 to 4 minutes.

Place the lamb on your smoke-roaster and smoke for about 2 hours or until the internal temperature reaches 130°F for medium-rare, or longer if desired. Serve with pumpkin seed sauce and roasted red onions, if you like.

Calf's Liver with Melon, Madeira, and Ham

Serves 8 to 10

1 honeydew or Cantaloupe melon
1½ cups Madeira wine
2 Tbsp cracked black pepper
1 Tbsp kosher salt
4 lb fresh calf's liver, cleaned, rolled,
  and tied
¼ cup Dijon mustard slather
  (see page 61)
6 to 8 slices bacon
6 shallots, minced
¼ cup balsamic vinegar
2 cups beef or chicken broth
1 stick sweet butter, cubed and chilled
2 Tbsp chopped fresh chives
½ lb ham, rind removed, sliced thin
  and diced

Spoon out some flesh from the melon and make a round indentation large enough to scrape or shake out the seeds. Pour some Madeira into the hole, replace the melon flesh on top, and chill overnight in the refrigerator.

Combine the pepper and salt and blend well. Coat the liver all over with mustard slather, season with the salt and pepper mixture, and lay the bacon slices on top. Place on the smoker, using apple wood. Smoke for 1 to 2 hours or until the internal temperature is between 120 and 130°F.

Remove the "plug" from the melon indentation, and pour the Madeira into a bowl and reserve. Peel and slice the melon. Cut into medium sized chunks and put into a bowl. Pour a small amount of the reserved Madeira over the melon, cover, set aside, and keep cool.

Place the shallots and vinegar in a saucepan over medium heat. Reduce by three-quarters, add the remaining reserved Madeira, and reduce to ¼ cup. Add the broth and reduce to about 1½ cups. Reduce the heat to a low simmer. Adjust the seasoning. Set aside and keep warm.

To serve, remove the strings and bacon from the liver. Slice into ¼-inch slices; place on a serving platter or plates.

Whisk the butter into the sauce until incorporated, pour the sauce over the meat, and garnish with melon, chopped chives, and diced ham.

Beef Brisket with Spicy Barbecue Rub and Angel's Mustard Slather

Serves 8 to 10

One 4- to 8-lb beef brisket

FOR THE SPICY
BARBECUE RUB

¼ cup cane sugar
1 Tbsp garlic salt
1 Tbsp celery salt
1 Tbsp hickory salt
1 Tbsp barbecue spice
2 Tbsp paprika
1 Tbsp chili powder
1 Tbsp fine ground black pepper
1 tsp celery seeds
1 tsp chipotle powder
½ tsp cayenne
¼ tsp ground cloves

FOR THE ANGEL'S
MUSTARD SLATHER

2 tsp granulated garlic
1 tsp granulated onion
1 tsp fine ground black pepper
½ tsp cayenne
½ tsp white pepper
½ tsp sea salt
2 Tbsp soy sauce
2 Tbsp white wine
2 Tbsp Worcestershire sauce
1 cup Dijon mustard

Trim the fat from the brisket leaving a ¼ to ⅛-inch fat cap. Trim the fat pockets even with the side of the brisket. Cover and set aside.

For the rub, combine the sugar, garlic salt, celery salt, hickory salt, barbecue spice, paprika, chili powder, black pepper, celery seeds, chipotle powder, cayenne, and cloves and blend well. Store in an airtight container in a cool dry place.

To make the angel's mustard slather, add the garlic, onion, peppers and salt to a nonreactive bowl. Blend in the soy sauce, white wine, and Worcestershire sauce and dissolve the spices with a wire whisk. Stir in the mustard and incorporate all the ingredients.

Using a pastry brush, cover the lean side of the meat with the mustard slather. Season with the rub, sprinkle on salt and pepper and do not rub in. Turn the brisket and repeat the process on the fat side. Place on your cooker and smoke for 8 to 12 hours or until a skewer inserted in the flat part of the brisket, against the grain, goes in easily and comes out with no resistance.

Beef Tenderloin
with Raspberry Ginger Sauce and Garlic Smashed Potatoes

Serves 8 to 10

FOR THE SEASONING

¼ cup dried brown sugar
2 Tbsp garlic salt
2 Tbsp onion salt
2 Tbsp paprika
1 Tbsp chili powder
1 Tbsp black pepper
1 tsp cayenne
½ tsp dried oregano
½ tsp ground ginger
½ tsp ground coriander
¼ tsp celery seeds

**One 4- to 5-lb beef-tenderloin,
  trimmed of membrane and fat**
¼ cup olive oil

Combine the sugar, garlic salt, onion salt, paprika, chili powder, pepper, cayenne, oregano, ginger, coriander, and celery seeds in a bowl and mix well. Store in an airtight container in a cool dry place.

Rub the trimmed tenderloin all over with the olive oil and season all over with the beef seasoning. Place on your cooker and smoke with fruitwood for 1 to 3 hours or until the tenderloin reaches 130°F for medium-rare, or longer if desired.

Raspberry ginger sauce

2 cups catsup
3 Tbsp grated gingerroot
4 cloves garlic, minced
1½ cups Melba sauce
   (raspberry sauce)
¼ cup brown sugar
¼ cup liquid honey
¼ cup fresh orange juice
2 Tbsp Grand Marnier or
   Cointreau

2 Tbsp Worcestershire sauce
2 Tbsp soy sauce
2 Tbsp cider vinegar
1 Tbsp orange zest
2 scallions, chopped
2 tsp ground chipotle pepper
1 tsp ground allspice
1 tsp sea salt

While the meat is cooking make the sauce. Combine the catsup, ginger, garlic, Melba sauce, sugar, honey, orange juice, Grand Marnier or Cointreau, Worcestershire sauce, soy sauce, vinegar, orange zest, scallions, ground chipotle, allspice, and salt in a saucepan and bring to a boil, stirring constantly. Reduce the heat and simmer, stirring occasionally, for 30 minutes. Strain and discard the scallions. Serve hot.

Serve the meat with the raspberry ginger sauce on the side and accompany with garlic mashed potatoes.

Garlic smashed potatoes

4 whole heads garlic, tops removed
½ cup olive oil
5 lb Yukon Gold or floury potatoes
1 Tbsp sea salt
1 stick butter
2 cups warm half-and-half
1 tsp sea salt
½ tsp white pepper

Pour the olive oil over the cut part of the garlic heads. Place on your smoker for about 2 hours or until the cloves are soft and tender. Remove the cloves from their skin, set aside 6 to 8 for the mashed potatoes, place the rest in a sterile jar, cover with a layer of olive oil, seal, and refrigerate. This smoke-roasted garlic will last for about 1 week in the refrigerator.

Wash the potatoes, place in a large pot, and cover with cold water and 1 tablespoon sea salt. Bring to a boil. Reduce the heat and simmer until tender. Drain the potatoes and place in a bowl. Add the reserved cloves of smoke-roasted garlic, butter, and warm half-and-half, and mash to the desired texture. Season to taste.

Pastrami with Irish Whiskey Sauce

Serves 6 to 8

One 4-lb brisket flat or eye-of-round roast

FOR THE BRINING OR CURE

1 cup sea salt
¹/₂ cup cane sugar
¹/₄ cup Morton Tender Quick
2 quarts water
2 Tbsp pickling spice
2 tsp whole black peppercorns
2 bay leaves, crumbled
2 cloves garlic, minced
1 to 2 cups coarse ground black pepper
1 cup coarse ground coriander

FOR THE SAUCE

1 cup Irish whiskey
1¹/₂ cups dark brown cane sugar
3 Tbsp Dijon mustard
³/₄ cup apple juice
1 tsp sea salt
1 Tbsp arrowroot
2 Tbsp cold water

Start brining the meat seven days before you intend to smoke it. Combine the salt, sugar, Tender Quick, water, pickling spice, peppercorns, bay leaf, and garlic, in a large nonreactive bowl or stockpot. Place the beef in the brine and weight it down, making sure that it is always submerged. Cover and refrigerate for seven days. Turn the beef at least once a day. Remove the beef from the brine and rinse with cold water. Combine the pepper and coriander in a small bowl and blend well. Press the pepper-coriander mixture into the beef. Place the beef on your cooker and smoke for 4 to 10 hours or until a skewer can be inserted easily against the grain and comes out easily. The reason for the large variance in time is because if you use inside or eye-of-round you could be done in 4 hours, whereas brisket flats can take 7 to 10 hours.

In a saucepan combine the whiskey, brown sugar, apple juice, and salt over medium heat and simmer, stirring with a wire whisk. In a small bowl combine the arrowroot and cold water and blend into a paste. Stir in the sauce, stirring until thickened. Serve the sauce hot, on the side.

SMOKED LAMB
WITH RED PEPPER RELISH

Serves 6 to 8

One 7- to 9-lb leg of lamb, trimmed

FOR THE MARINADE

2 cups chopped onions
1 cup red wine
½ cup liquid honey
¼ cup Worcestershire sauce
¼ cup sunflower oil
8 cloves garlic, chopped
1 tsp sea salt
1 tsp black pepper

Combine the onions, wine, honey, Worcestershire sauce, oil, garlic, salt, and pepper in a blender fitted with a steel blade. Purée until smooth. Place the lamb in a zip-lock type plastic bag. Pour the marinade over it and seal. Marinate for 7 to 8 hours in the refrigerator or overnight.

To cook, remove the lamb from the marinade and smoke for about 4 hours or until the internal temperature reaches 130°F for medium-rare, or longer if desired. Allow to rest for 10 to 15 minutes. Carve and serve with red pepper relish.

Red pepper relish

4 cups diced sweet red peppers
2 cups diced Spanish or red onions
2 cups cider vinegar
1 cup sugar
1 Tbsp crushed red peppers
2 tsp yellow mustard seeds
2 tsp sea salt

In a heavy saucepan add the peppers, onions, vinegar, sugar, crushed red peppers, mustard seeds, and salt over medium heat. Simmer, stirring occasionally, about 1 hour or until the mixture has reduced to about 3 cups. Serve the relish chilled or at room temperature.

Smoked Lamb with Red Pepper Relish

Venison with Wild Mushroom Sauce

Serves 6 to 8

¼ cup bacon drippings
2 Tbsp yellow mustard
4 large cloves smoke-roasted garlic
   (see page 73), minced
2 tsp coarse ground black pepper
1 tsp kosher salt
One 3- to 4-lb venison strip loin

FOR THE SAUCE

3 to 4 oz dried porcini mushrooms
2 quarts water
1 cup Madeira wine
2 sticks sweet butter, one stick cut
   into cubes and frozen
1 lb assorted fresh, wild, and
   cultivated mushrooms, stemmed
   and sliced thin
¼ to ⅓ cup tomato paste
1 tsp sea salt
1 tsp fresh ground black pepper

Combine the bacon drippings, mustard, garlic, pepper, and salt in a small bowl, blending well with a wire whisk. Rub the mixture all over the venison, wrap in plastic wrap or place in a nonreactive baking pan, cover, and marinate overnight in the refrigerator. Place on the cooker and smoke at least 250°F for 2 to 3 hours. Do not overcook, rare and medium-rare are the acceptable doneness range for venison.

In a large saucepan, combine the dried mushrooms and the water. Cook over high heat for 30 to 35 minutes. Strain through cheesecloth and squeeze the liquid from the mushrooms to extract all the juice and flavor. Discard the mushrooms and return the broth to the pan. Add the Madeira and bring to a boil. Reduce to 1½ to 2 cups.

Melt one stick butter in a large skillet over medium heat and sauté the fresh mushrooms until tender, about 5 minutes. Set aside.

Over medium heat, add the tomato paste to the reduced mushroom liquid and blend with a wire whisk until smooth. Blend in the frozen butter cubes over low heat until they are all incorporated. Add the sautéed mushrooms, salt, and pepper. Set aside and keep warm.

Slice the venison into medallions and top with a little sauce. Serve the remaining sauce on the side.

Smoked Black Bean Duck
with Spicy Lo-mein

Serves 2 to 4

One 3½- to 4½-lb duckling
½ cup soy sauce
3 Tbsp fermented black beans, crushed
3 Tbsp dark brown sugar
4 cloves garlic, minced
2 tsp ground cinnamon
½ tsp Chinese five-spice powder
½ cup diced scallions

FOR THE MARINADE
AND BASTE

1 cup soy sauce
1 Tbsp sugar
2 tsp grated gingerroot
1 tsp garlic, minced

Wash and rinse the duck, and pat dry with paper towels. Tie the neck with string, or secure with skewers to seal it. Combine the soy sauce, black beans, sugar, garlic, cinnamon, five-spice powder, and scallions in a bowl and blend well. Pour into the body cavity of the duck. Insert skewers across the opening and lace tightly with string to prevent the sauce from oozing out.

For the marinade, combine the soy sauce, sugar, gingerroot, and garlic in a bowl and blend well with a wire whisk.

Place the duck in a heavy-duty plastic bag and pour the marinade over. Press all the air out of the bag and tie it with string. Marinate the duck in the refrigerator for 3 to 4 hours or overnight.

Remove the duck from the marinade, reserving it to use as a baste. Place the duck on your cooker and smoke for 2 to 3 hours at 250°F, basting the duck about every 30 minutes with the reserved marinade. If you prefer your duck rare reduce the cooking time in half.

Spicy lo-mein

Serves 4 to 6

¼ cup peanut oil
3 cloves garlic, minced
1 Tbsp grated gingerroot
1 to 2 tsp crushed red peppers
¼ cup scallions, cut on a bias
¼ cup bamboo shoots, sliced
¼ cup sliced celery
¼ cup shredded onions
¼ cup sliced mushrooms
½ cup bean sprouts
½ lb noodles, such as linguine or spaghetti, cooked
3 Tbsp soy sauce
1 Tbsp cane sugar
1 Tbsp sherry
2 tsp sesame oil
1 tsp fresh ground black pepper
½ tsp sea salt

Add the peanut oil to a large skillet or wok and heat until almost smoking. Add the garlic, gingerroot, and crushed red peppers and sauté or stir-fry for about 1 minute until fragrant. Combine the scallions, bamboo shoots, celery, onions, and mushrooms; add to the wok or skillet and stir-fry for 2 to 3 minutes. Add the bean sprouts and cook for about 1 minute. Add the noodles and cook for 1 to 2 minutes or until warm. Combine the soy sauce, sherry, sesame oil, pepper, and salt and add to the vegetable-noodle mixture and toss to blend.

BEER-MARINATED CHICKEN

Serves 4 to 8

FOR THE BEER MARINADE	FOR THE SPICY BARBECUED CHICKEN RUB
2 cups bottled Italian salad dressing	½ cup cane sugar
12 oz flat beer from 2 cans of beer, reserving ½ of each beer	⅓ cup celery salt
4 large cloves garlic, minced	⅓ cup onion salt
2 Tbsp grated onions	2 Tbsp garlic salt
2 Tbsp cane sugar	⅓ cup paprika
1 Tbsp coarse ground black pepper	1 Tbsp chili powder
2 tsp kosher salt	2 tsp lemon pepper
1 tsp grated lemon zest	2 tsp fine ground black pepper
1 tsp fresh tarragon leaves	1 to 2 tsp cayenne
	1 tsp rubbed sage
	1 tsp dried basil leaves
2 whole 3- to 4-lb chickens	1 tsp dried tarragon leaves

Combine the salad dressing, beer, garlic, onion, sugar, pepper, salt, lemon zest, and tarragon in a bowl and blend well with a wire whisk.

Rinse the chicken with cold water; remove the giblets and reserve for another purpose or discard. Pat dry with paper towels. Place the chickens in a heavy plastic bag and pour the marinade over them, remove all of the air in the bag, and tie shut. Marinate the chickens for 4 hours in the refrigerator.

Combine the sugar, celery salt, onion salt, garlic salt, paprika, chili powder, lemon pepper, pepper, cayenne to taste, sage, basil, and tarragon in a bowl and blend well.

Remove the chickens from the marinade, lightly pat dry with paper towels, and season inside and out with the rub. Place the chicken on the upright half-full beer cans, positioning the legs out in front, and put in your cooker. Smoke-roast for about 4 hours or until the internal temperature is 160°F or until the juices run clear.

Beer-marinated Chicken

TANDOORI CHICKEN BREASTS

Serves 6

FOR THE MARINADE

$\frac{1}{8}$ tsp saffron threads
2 Tbsp boiling water
1 cup plain yogurt
2 Tbsp fresh lemon juice
2 Tbsp white wine vinegar
1 Tbsp paprika
2 tsp grated gingerroot
3 cloves garlic, minced
1 jalapeño chile, seeded and minced
1 tsp toasted ground cumin
1 tsp ground coriander
1 tsp curry powder
1 tsp cayenne
1 tsp salt
$\frac{1}{2}$ tsp ground cinnamon
$\frac{1}{2}$ tsp chili powder

Six 5-oz boneless, skinless chicken breasts

Dissolve the saffron in a small bowl with the boiling water. Combine the yogurt, lemon juice, vinegar, paprika, ginger, garlic, jalapeño chile, cumin, coriander, curry powder, cayenne, salt, cinnamon, and chili powder in a nonreactive bowl and blend well with a wire whisk. Add the saffron and blend in.

Dip the chicken breasts into the marinade, covering on all sides, place in a glass baking pan, cover, and marinate for 2 to 4 hours in the refrigerator. Place on your cooker and smoke for about 1 hour or until the internal temperature reaches 160°F. Serve with steamed rice.

SWEET AND SPICY ROCK CORNISH HENS

Serves 8

4 rock Cornish hens, halved

FOR THE MARINADE

One 30-oz can plums, drained and pitted
1 onion, diced
2 cloves garlic, minced
¼ cup red wine
¼ cup teriyaki sauce
2 Tbsp chili sauce
Juice of 1 lemon
2 tsp sesame oil
1 tsp salt
½ tsp black pepper

Rinse the rock Cornish hens in cold water and pat dry with paper towels. Make several deep slashes in the flesh of each hen half. Set aside. Place all the ingredients, except the hen halves, in a food processor or blender. Process until smooth. Place the hens cut-side down in a nonreactive dish. Pour over the marinade. Cover and marinate in the refrigerator, turning and basting frequently, for at least 24 hours. Drain the hens, reserving the marinade. Place the hens on your cooker and smoke for 3 to 4 hours or until the internal temperature is 160°F or the juices run clear.

BARBECUED CHICKEN

Serves 6 to 8

FOR THE MARINADE

½ cup sunflower oil
⅓ cup soy sauce
¼ cup Worcestershire sauce
¼ cup red wine vinegar
2 Tbsp fresh lemon juice
1 Tbsp dry mustard
1 Tbsp fresh parsley, minced
1 tsp fresh basil leaves, minced
2 large cloves garlic, minced
1 tsp sea salt
1 tsp fresh ground black pepper

2 whole 4- to 5-lb chickens

Combine the oil, soy sauce, Worcestershire sauce, vinegar, lemon juice, mustard, parsley, basil, garlic, salt, and pepper in a nonreactive bowl and blend well with a wire whisk. Cut the chicken into portions. Place in a zip-lock type plastic bag and pour the marinade over it. Marinate for 2 to 4 hours. Remove the chicken from the marinade, reserving it. Place the chicken on your cooker and cook for 2 to 5 hours or until the internal temperature is 160°F. After 1½ hours baste with the reserved marinade every 30 minutes.

Sweet and Spicy Rock Cornish Hens

SMOKED CHICKEN LIVERS

**Serves 8 as an entrée,
15 to 20 as an appetizer**

FOR THE BARBECUE
SEASONING

**2 Tbsp dried brown cane sugar
2 Tbsp white cane sugar
1 Tbsp garlic salt
1 Tbsp seasoned salt
1 Tbsp celery salt
2 Tbsp paprika
1 Tbsp chili powder
1 Tbsp lemon pepper
½ tsp ground chipotle powder
½ tsp dry mustard
½ tsp ground ginger
¼ tsp ground allspice
⅛ tsp mace**

**80 chicken livers
Nonstick cooking spray or olive oil**

Combine the dried brown sugar, sugar, garlic salt, seasoned salt, celery salt, paprika, chili powder, lemon pepper, chipotle powder, mustard, ginger, allspice, and mace in a bowl and blend well. Store in an airtight container in a cool dry place.

Soak 8 wooden skewers in water for 30 minutes. Thread 10 livers on each skewer, coat with nonstick spray or oil, and season to taste with the barbecue seasoning. Place on your smoker and smoke for about 1 hour, being careful not to overcook beyond 120°F if using a thermometer. Serve with your favorite salsa.

Cajun-marinated Turkey Kabobs

Serves 6 to 8

1 to 2 lb turkey tenderloin cut into
   1-in cubes
1 lb smoked or Polish Kielbasa
   sausage, cut into chunks
2 large sweet red peppers, seeded
   and cut into 1-in pieces
1 large onion cut into 1-in pieces

FOR THE MARINADE

1 cup Dijon mustard
1/2 cup fresh lemon juice
1/4 cup Cajun seasoning
1 fl. oz garlic, minced
1/4 cup white wine
1/4 cup olive oil
1 Tbsp kosher salt

Combine all the ingredients in a bowl and blend well with a wire whisk. Cover and marinate the turkey overnight in the refrigerator.

Thread the turkey, sausage, pepper, and onion onto 8 skewers. Place on the cooker and smoke for 2 to 3 hours until the internal temperature is 160°F.

Curry Chicken with Coconut Sauce

Serves 6

FOR THE CURRY RUB

1/4 cup cane sugar
2 Tbsp curry powder
1 Tbsp garlic salt
 2 tsp toasted ground cumin
1 tsp fine ground black pepper
1 tsp ground turmeric
1 tsp cayenne
1/2 tsp ground cardamom

Six 5-oz boneless, skinless chicken
   breasts

FOR THE SAUCE

1/2 stick butter
1 cup diced onions
4 large cloves garlic, minced
1 to 2 Serrano chiles, seeded and
   minced
1/4 cup chicken broth
1 cup coconut milk
1 tsp sea salt

Combine the sugar, curry powder, salt, cumin, pepper, turmeric, cayenne, and cardamom in a bowl and blend well. Store in an airtight container in a cool dark place.

Season the chicken breasts on all sides with the curry rub and place on a plate. Cover with plastic wrap and marinate for 1 to 2 hours in the refrigerator. Place on your cooker and smoke for 1 to 2 hours or until the internal temperature is 160°F.

Melt the butter in a medium saucepan over medium high heat and add the onions, garlic, and chiles. Sauté, stirring, until soft, about 4 to 5 minutes. Add the broth and simmer for 2 minutes. Add the coconut milk and salt. Simmer for 5 minutes. Set aside and keep warm. Serve over the chicken.

Achiote-marinated Quail with Salad and Papaya-Chile Vinaigrette

Serves 2 to 4

8 quail, dressed

FOR THE ACHIOTE MARINADE

1 cup olive oil
1/4 cup achiote (or annato) seeds or 1
    tsp each tumeric and mild paprika
1 clove garlic, minced
1 tsp sea salt
1/2 tsp white pepper
Assorted green salad leaves

FOR THE VINAIGRETTE

1 roasted Serrano chile, peeled,
    seeded, and minced
1 small papaya, peeled, seeded, and
    diced
1 cup olive oil
1/4 cup Champagne vinegar

Heat the olive oil in a small saucepan until warm. Stir in the achiote seeds, garlic, salt, and pepper and remove from heat (if using tumeric and paprika, add after you have removed the oil from the heat). Allow to cool.

Place the quail in a nonreactive bowl or dish and pour the marinade over them, making sure all are coated. Cover and marinate for 1 to 3 hours in the refrigerator.

Remove the quail from the marinade; reserve the marinade to baste with. Place the quail on your cooker and smoke for 1 to 2 hours, until tender, basting with the reserved marinade.

To make the vinaigrette, combine the Serrano and papaya in a bowl and mix well. Place half of the chile-papaya mixture in a bowl with the olive oil and vinegar and blend well. Reserve the other half of the mixture.

To serve, place 2 quail on a serving plate with salad topped with vinaigrette. Garnish with the rest of the chile-papaya mixture.

Southwestern Orange Roughy

Serves 4 to 6

1/2 cup sour cream
1/2 cup cream cheese, softened
1 cup grated Cheddar cheese
1 Tbsp grated onion
1 Tbsp fresh lime juice
1/2 tsp toasted ground cumin
1/2 tsp granulated garlic
1/2 tsp sea salt
1/4 tsp white pepper
1/4 tsp cayenne
2 lb orange roughy fillets, cut into
    serving portions
Paprika, cilantro sprigs, sliced
    pickled jalapeño chiles to garnish

Combine the sour cream and cream cheese and blend until smooth. Add the Cheddar cheese, onion, and lime juice and blend in until smooth as possible. Blend in the cumin, garlic, salt, white pepper, and cayenne until smooth. Spread the mixture evenly over the fillets and place on your cooker. Smoke for 30 to 45 minutes or until the fish flakes easily. Carefully remove the fillets with a spatula, being careful not to lose any of the cheese mixture on top. Garnish with paprika, cilantro sprigs, and slices of jalapeño chile. Heat any leftover mixture in a small saucepan until soft and warm, serve on the side.

Achiote-marinated Quail

FIVE-PEPPER PHEASANT

Serves 4 to 6

FOR THE FIVE-PEPPER
SEASONING

2 Tbsp raw sugar
1 Tbsp kosher salt
2 tsp coarse ground Szechuan
   pepper
2 tsp coarse ground black
   peppercorns
2 tsp coarse ground pink
   peppercorns
2 tsp coarse ground green
   peppercorns
2 tsp coarse ground allspice
1 tsp coarse ground white
   peppercorns

2 oranges, halved
2 young 3½-lb pheasants, dressed
10 to 12 slices bacon

Combine the sugar, salt, Szechuan pepper, black pepper, pink pepper-corns, green peppercorns, allspice, and white pepper in a small bowl and blend well.

Cut the oranges in half and rub over the outside of the pheasants. Season inside and out with the pepper seasoning. Place the orange halves inside the pheasants. Cover the breast and legs with the bacon. Place on the cooker and smoke at at least 250°F for 2 to 3 hours, until the internal temperature is 160°F or until the juices run clear. Baste the pheasants with apple juice as they cook.

SMOKED OYSTERS ROCKEFELLER

Serves 24

½ stick butter
⅓ cup scallions, sliced thin
2 large cloves garlic, minced
One 10-oz package frozen chopped
   spinach, defrosted and drained
1 Tbsp dry sherry
1 tsp sea salt
1 tsp fresh ground pepper
¼ cup fine dried bread crumbs
2 dozen oysters on the half shell,
   grained
2 Tbsp fresh lemon juice
Hot sauce
4 slices bacon, fried crisp and
   crumbled
24 strips smoked roasted red
   pepper

Heat the butter in a saucepan over medium-high heat, add the onions and garlic, and sauté until tender, about 3 minutes. Stir in the spinach, sherry, salt, and pepper and cook for a further 3 minutes. Remove from the heat and stir in the bread crumbs. Place each oyster on a canning screwtop lid, and top each with some lemon juice and hot sauce. Top with the spinach mixture and garnish with bacon and red pepper strips. Place in your cooker and smoke for 20 minutes to 1 hour.

Five-pepper Pheasant

Barbecued Coho Salmon
with Lemon Rice Stuffing

Serves 6 to 8

FOR THE WHITE WINE MARINADE

1½ cups dry vermouth
½ cup fresh lemon juice
½ cup olive oil
½ cup grated onions
4 large cloves garlic, minced
1 Tbsp grated gingerroot
1 Tbsp dill
1 Tbsp hot sauce
1 tsp fresh thyme leaves, minced
1 tsp sea salt
1 tsp fine ground black pepper

Two 2-lb coho salmon

Combine the vermouth, lemon juice, olive oil, onion, garlic, gingerroot dill, hot sauce, thyme, salt, and pepper in a bowl and blend well with a wire whisk. With a sharp knife score both sides of the fish by making four or five evenly spaced slits about 1 to 2 inches long and about ¼ inch deep. Place the fish in a nonreactive baking pan or plastic bag and pour the marinade over the fish. Cover and marinate for 2 hours in the refrigerator. Turn the fish every 30 minutes to coat well.

Place the fish upright on your cooker so the skewers will hold it up. With a pastry brush, cover with olive oil and season with the dill. Smoke-roast for 1 to 2 hours using apple, alder, or pecan wood, basting with the marinade as you cook, until the fish flakes easily.

Lemon rice stuffing

1 cup freshly cooked rice, cooled
¼ cup fine sliced scallions
   (white and green)
¼ cup fresh parsley, minced
½ lemon, seeded and minced
   (include the peel)
1 Tbsp grated lemon zest
¼ cup olive oil
2 Tbsp dill

For the stuffing combine the rice, scallions, parsley, lemon, and lemon zest and blend well. Remove the fish from the marinade, drain on paper towels, and pat dry. Strain the marinade, add ¼ cup to the stuffing, and blend well. Reserve the excess marinade. Lightly insert the stuffing into the fish cavities. Using 3 to 5 bamboo skewers per fish, skewer each fish cavity 1 inch from the front opening, breast area and 1 inch from the rear end, with another in the middle. Secure with a double length of string.

SMOKED TROUT WITH SEASONED COUSCOUS AND BALSAMIC SMOKE-ROASTED ONIONS

Serves 4

Two 2-lb rainbow or brown trout
½ cup sunflower oil
2 Tbsp kosher salt
1 Tbsp lemon pepper

Rub the fish all over, inside and out with the oil. Combine the salt and lemon pepper in a small bowl and blend well. Season the fish inside and out with the mixture. To place the fish on your cooker, turn the belly flaps out as the base and set the fish up. Smoke for 1 to 2 hours or until the fish flakes easily. To serve, spoon couscous on a serving platter, top with the fish, and place the onions around the edge.

Seasoned couscous

1 Tbsp peanut oil
6 scallions, sliced thin
  (green and white)
2 cloves garlic, minced
¾ cup water
1 Tbsp chicken-flavored bouillon
  granules
½ cup couscous
1 Tbsp light soy sauce
½ cup Roma tomatoes, peeled,
  seeded and chopped
1 Tbsp fresh parsley, minced
1 tsp fresh ground black pepper

Add the peanut oil to a saucepan over a medium heat and sauté the scallions and garlic until tender, about 2 to 3 minutes. Add the water and bouillon and bring to a boil. Remove from the heat. Stir in the couscous and soy sauce, cover, and allow to stand for 5 minutes. Stir in the tomatoes, parsley, and pepper. Cover and set aside.

Balsamic smoked-roasted onions

¼ cup olive oil
3 Tbsp balsamic vinegar
3 Tbsp cane sugar
2 Tbsp soy sauce
2 large red onions, cut into wedges

Combine the olive oil, balsamic vinegar, sugar, and soy sauce in a large bowl and blend well with a wire whisk until the sugar dissolves. Add the onion wedges and toss to coat. Pour all of the ingredients in a shallow 9 x 13-inch baking pan and place on your cooker. Smoke-roast, stirring every 20 minutes, for 2 hours or until the onions are soft and coated with a thick glaze.

Swordfish with Herbs, Smoked Bacon, and Red Wine Butter Sauce

Serves 6 to 8

3 lb swordfish
1/2 lb slab bacon, rind removed, cut into matchstick pieces
1/2 cup fresh basil leaves, chopped
1/4 cup fresh thyme leaves
1/4 cup fresh chervil leaves, chopped
1/4 cup fresh tarragon leaves
1/4 cup olive oil
5 cloves garlic, minced
1 Tbsp kosher salt
1 Tbsp fresh coarse ground black pepper

FOR THE SAUCE

1/4 cup minced shallots
1 Tbsp olive oil
1/2 cup red wine vinegar
1 tsp cracked black pepper
1 bay leaf
1 cup red wine
1 cup heavy cream
2 sticks sweet butter, cut into small pieces and kept cold

Have your fishmonger cut an even-sized section of fresh boneless, skinless swordfish. Divide in half.

Sauté the bacon in a large skillet until medium-rare. Remove and drain on paper towels. Sauté the herbs over high heat for about 1 minute to wilt. Remove from the heat and drain.

Using a larding needle or sharp knife, insert the bacon evenly over both sections of the swordfish. Rub the olive oil all over the fish then rub the garlic over the top of the flesh. Season with the salt and pepper and top with the wilted herbs. Place in your cooker and smoke with the wood of your choice, for 1 to 1 1/2 hours or until the fish flakes easily.

In a medium saucepan, stew the shallots in 1 tablespoon olive oil. Add the vinegar, cracked black pepper, and bay leaf and reduce to about 3 tablespoons. Add the red wine and reduce to 1/4 cup. Add the heavy cream and reduce until it thickens. Beat in the butter, bit by bit, until it is all incorporated and strain through a cheesecloth or sieve. Keep warm.

Cut the swordfish into serving pieces. Place some sauce on the serving plates and top with the fish and serve. Garnish with lemon or lime wedges if liked.

ACCOMPANIMENTS AND DESSERTS

I THINK THE Pennsylvania Dutch have a great philosophy when planning meals, accompaniments, and what I call side dishes. They plan 7 sours and 7 sweets. When I plan a meal around smoked meats, the menu will consist bread, which can be plain bread, to French bread, or Italian, garlic bread or Brochette (my favorite along with cornbread). Since I like beans I plan either a hot style of beans or a cold style bean salad. As a general rule I pick at least 4 side dishes, not counting the bread, to go with my meal.

If I plan a dessert it is something light and fresh, such as chilled fresh fruit, sherbet, or maybe ice cream. If you have a favorite dish, you can experiement with the best smoked meats to complement it.

TABBOULEH

Serves 6 to 8

¾ cup bulgur wheat
2 cups boiling water
1 tsp sea salt
½ tsp ground allspice
1 cup diced red onions
2 cups fresh curly or flat-leaf
   parsley, minced
1½ cups diced cucumber, seeded
   and peeled
½ cup scallions, sliced thin
1 cup mint leaves, minced
¼ cup fresh lemon juice
¼ cup olive oil

Put the bulgur wheat in a heatproof bowl. Pour over the boiling water. Allow the bulgur to stand for 1 hour. In a large bowl stir together the red onions, salt, and allspice and allow to stand for 30 minutes. Drain the bulgur in a sieve, pressing hard to remove the excess water. Combine the drained bulgur, parsley, cucumber, scallions, and mint. Combine the lemon juice and oil and blend well. Pour over the bulgur mixture and toss. Cover and chill.

SMOKED POTATO SALAD

Serves 6 to 8

2 lb small red potatoes
1 Tbsp sea salt
¼ cup soy oil
8 to 10 slices bacon
6 scallions, sliced thin
2 Tbsp cider vinegar
3 Tbsp soy oil
1 clove garlic, minced
1 tsp sea salt
½ tsp white pepper

Rinse the potatoes of any dirt, place in a stockpot, and cover with cold water by 2 inches. Bring to a boil. Add the salt and simmer, covered, until the potatoes are just tender, 10 to 15 minutes. Drain in a colander and cool.

Cut the potatoes in half, place in a bowl and pour over ¼ cup oil. Toss to coat. Place in a smoker and smoke for 15 minutes to 1 hour, depending on the amount of smoke that you want and the smoking equipment you have.

Fry the bacon until crisp, reserving 2 tablespoons of the dripping, and drain on paper towels. Crumble or dice the bacon.

In a large bowl toss the potatoes with reserved drippings, bacon, scallions, vinegar, remaining oil, garlic, salt, and pepper.

Tabbouleh

RISOTTO WITH PANCETTA AND WILD MUSHROOMS

Serves 6 to 8

8 to 12 paper-thin slices pancetta
    or lean bacon
2 Tbsp extra-virgin olive oil
1 Tbsp sweet butter
1 lb mixed mushrooms, chanterelles,
    cremini, and Portobello, thick sliced
2 tsp sea salt
3 Tbsp sweet butter
1 tsp fresh tarragon leaves, minced
5 cups chicken broth
2 cloves garlic, minced
½ cup diced shallots
1½ cups arborio rice
½ cup grated Parmesan cheese
2 Tbsp whipping cream
1 tsp sea salt
1 tsp fresh ground white pepper
¼ cup shaved Parmesan cheese

Broil or bake the pancetta or bacon until crisp, drain on paper towels, then crumble. In a large nonstick skillet over medium-high heat add the olive oil and 1 tablespoon butter. Add the mushrooms, season with salt and sauté over a high heat until the mushrooms exude their juice, 3 to 5 minutes. Transfer the mushrooms and their liquid to a strainer, set over a bowl and press lightly on the mushrooms; Reserve the liquid. Add 1 tablespoon butter to a clean skillet over a medium heat and sauté, stirring, until tender and just beginning to brown, 2 to 3 minutes. Add the tarragon and set aside.

In a medium saucepan, combine the broth and mushroom liquid, bring to a simmer, and keep warm over a low heat. Melt 1 tablespoon butter in a deep nonstick skillet. Add the garlic and sauté, until just fragrant. Add the shallots and cook until soft but not browned, 3 to 4 minutes. Add the rice and stir until the grains are coated with butter. Add 1 cup of broth and cook, stirring constantly, until the broth is absorbed, 1 to 2 minutes. Continue to cook the risotto, adding 1 cup broth at a time, stirring constantly between additions, until it is absorbed. Cook until creamy consistency, about 20 minutes. Remove from the heat and stir in the Parmesan, cream, and remaining butter. Season with salt and pepper and transfer to a serving bowl. Garnish with pancetta, mushrooms, and shavings of Parmesan cheese. Serve immediately.

CANDIED YAMS OR SWEET POTATOES

Serves 4 to 6

4 medium yams or sweet potatoes
1 cup brown sugar
1 stick butter
About 1 quart water
1 tsp sea salt

Peel the potatoes and cut into 2-inch slices or chunks. Put the cut potatoes in a wide, heavy skillet. Add water to a quarter of the way up the sides of the skillet, cover, and cook slowly until they can be pierced with a fork. Remove from the heat and drain the water from the pan. Sprinkle the sugar over the potatoes, add butter and salt, and return to low heat. Cook, uncovered, until the liquid is sticky.

WHEAT BERRY WALDORF SALAD

Serves 6 to 8

1 cup wheat berries (whole-grain, hard wheat)

1 quart water

1 tsp sea salt

1 cup diced McIntosh apple

1 cup diced Granny Smith apple

1 quart water mixed with 2 Tbsp lemon juice

½ cup diced celery

½ cup dried sour cherries

¼ cup golden raisins

¼ cup fresh mint leaves, minced

4 scallions, sliced thin

¼ cup seasoned rice wine vinegar

3 Tbsp fresh orange juice

1 tsp grated orange zest

1 tsp sea salt

½ tsp white pepper

2 Tbsp walnuts, toasted and chopped

In a saucepan bring the water and salt to a boil and add the wheat berries. Reduce the heat and simmer, covered, for 1½ hours or until tender. Drain the wheat berries in a colander and cool to room temperature. Place the apples in the lemon water and set aside. Combine the celery, cherries, raisins, mint, and scallions in a large bowl. In another bowl combine the vinegar, orange juice, and orange zest. Drain the apples and add them to the celery mixture. Add the cooled wheat berries. Pour the orange juice mixture over the wheat berries and toss until well blended. Season with salt and pepper and garnish with toasted walnuts.

White Bean and Red Onion Salad

Serves 8 to 10

2 cups dried Great Northern or
    other white beans
1 Tbsp coarse ground coriander
2 bay leaves
2 tsp fresh ground black pepper

FOR THE DRESSING

4 cloves garlic, pressed
¼ cup fresh lemon juice
½ cup olive oil
2 tsp sea salt
2 cups diced red onions
¼ cup fresh cilantro, minced
¼ cup fresh parsley, minced

Rinse the beans with cold water. Add the beans to a stockpot with the coriander, bay leaves, and black pepper. Cover with cold water about 2 inches above. Simmer the beans, stirring occasionally. If necessary, add hot water as the cooking proceeds to keep the beans covered. Simmer for 1 to 1½ hours or until beans are tender but not mushy.

Combine the garlic and lemon juice and beat in the olive oil with a wire whisk, until well blended.

Drain the beans in a colander and discard the bay leaves. Add the beans to a large bowl and pour over the dressing. Toss and season with salt. Allow the salad to cool then stir in the onions, cilantro, and parsley.

Broccoli, Bacon, and Onion Salad

Serves 6 to 8

10 to 12 slices bacon
⅔ cup olive oil
3 Tbsp red wine vinegar
1 cup diced red onions
5 cups broccoli florets, blanched
    and chilled
1 cup raisins, soaked in hot water
    and chilled
½ cup sunflower seeds, toasted
1 tsp cane sugar
1 tsp sea salt
1 tsp coarse ground black pepper

Fry the bacon until crisp and drain on paper towels. Whisk the oil and vinegar in a medium bowl to blend. Mix in the onions. Combine the broccoli, raisins, and sunflower seeds and gently toss to blend. Season with sugar, salt, and pepper. Pour the dressing over the salad and toss to coat evenly. Crumble the bacon over the top of the salad and serve.

White Bean and Red Onion Salad

HONEY RED CABBAGE

Serves 6 to 8

3 Tbsp sunflower oil

1 large onion, sliced thin

3 large cloves garlic, minced

1 medium red cabbage, shredded
and chopped

2 Granny Smith apples, quartered,
cored, and thin sliced

2 Tbsp white wine vinegar

1 Tbsp cane sugar

2 Tbsp fresh dill

1/4 cup liquid honey

1 tsp sea salt

1 tsp fresh ground black pepper

Heat the oil in a large heavy skillet. Add the onions and sauté until soft, about 3 to 4 minutes. Add the garlic and cook for a further minute. Stir in the cabbage and cook, covered, for about 4 minutes or until the cabbage has wilted. Add the apples, vinegar, sugar, and dill. Stir well and continue to cook until the apples are tender, 7 to 8 minutes. Stir in honey, season with salt and pepper, and cook for a further 2 minutes.

BUTTERMILK COLESLAW

Serves 6 to 8

1 medium green cabbage, shredded
and chopped

2 cups diced onions

1 cup diced green bell pepper

1 cup diced sweet red pepper

1 cup celery, sliced thin

1/2 cup grated carrots

1 cup buttermilk

1/2 cup mayonnaise

1 tsp celery seeds

1 tsp sea salt

1/2 tsp white pepper

Combine the cabbage, onion, green bell pepper, sweet red pepper, celery, and carrot to a large bowl and gently toss. In another bowl add the buttermilk, mayonnaise, celery seeds, salt, and pepper and blend well with a wire whisk. Pour over the cabbage mixture and blend well. Cover and chill. Serve cold.

Honey Red Cabbage

Smoked Corn on the Cob with Flavored Butters

Serves 4 to 8

8 large ears fresh corn, with husk
  and silk left intact
1 gallon water
2 sticks butter or flavored butters
Salt and pepper to taste

Cut any corn silk sticking out of the top of the ear. Place the ears in a large bucket and pour over water. Weight the ears down with a weighted plate, keeping the ears submerged. Soak the corn for at least 8 hours, longer if possible. To cook place in a smoke-roaster and cook for at least 2 hours. It is difficult to overcook the corn because the wet husk protects it. To serve, peel or shuck the corn and smear with plain or flavored butter, salt, and pepper to taste.

Sun-dried tomato butter

1 stick sweet butter, softened
1 clove garlic, minced
2 tsp fresh lemon juice
$\frac{1}{2}$ tsp sea salt
2 Tbsp oil-packed sun-dried
  tomatoes, drained and fine
  minced
$\frac{1}{4}$ cup cilantro, minced
1 plum tomato, peeled, seeded, and
  minced

Place the butter, garlic, lemon juice, salt, sun-dried tomatoes, cilantro, and fresh tomato in a small bowl, and beat until well blended. Place in a small serving bowl. Serve at room temperature.

Ancho-avocado butter

2 Tbsp fresh lime juice
2 Tbsp water
1 small ripe avocado, peeled,
  seeded, and chopped
1 stick sweet butter, softened
1 small ancho chile, stemmed
  and seeded
1 tsp grated lime zest
1 tsp sea salt
$\frac{1}{2}$ tsp white pepper

Combine the lime juice and water in a small bowl. Add the diced avocado to the lime water. In another small bowl combine the butter, ancho chile, lime zest, salt, and pepper and blend well. Add the avocado and blend in until incorporated. Place in a small bowl. Serve the butter at room temperature.

Mixed herb butter

1 stick sweet butter, softened
2 Tbsp fresh flat-leaf parsley, minced
2 Tbsp fresh watercress leaves, minced
1 Tbsp fresh mint leaves, minced
1 Tbsp freshly grated Parmesan cheese
1 tsp fresh tarragon leaves, minced
1 tsp Pernod
1 tsp grated lemon zest
$\frac{1}{2}$ tsp hot sauce
$\frac{1}{2}$ tsp sea salt
$\frac{1}{4}$ tsp white pepper

Place the butter, parsley, watercress, mint, Parmesan cheese, tarragon, Pernod, lemon zest, hot sauce, salt, and pepper in a small bowl, and beat until well blended. Serve at room temperature.

CUCUMBER AND DILL SALAD

Serves 6 to 8

4 medium cucumbers, peeled and thin sliced
Juice of 2 lemons
1 tsp sea salt
1 cup sour cream
6 scallions, thin sliced
$\frac{1}{2}$ tsp white pepper
2 tsp fresh dill
1 tsp cane sugar

Place the cucumbers in a nonreactive bowl, squeeze over the lemon juice with $\frac{1}{2}$ teaspoon salt and gently toss. Cover and chill in the refrigerator for 30 minutes. Blend the sour cream, onions, remaining salt, pepper, and dill in a small bowl. Drain the cucumbers in a colander. Put the cucumbers back in the bowl. Fold the sour cream mixture into the cucumbers. Taste and adjust the seasoning with salt, pepper, lemon juice, and sugar.

SOUTHERN CORNBREAD

Serves 8

¼ cup bacon drippings
1½ cups self-rising corn meal
½ cup self-rising flour
1 large egg
1 cup whole milk

Preheat the oven to 500°F. Pour the bacon grease in a 9-inch cast-iron skillet or a 9-inch square baking pan and heat in the oven for 3 to 4 minutes.

Mix the corn meal, flour, egg, and milk in a small bowl with a wire whisk or a fork. Remove the skillet from the oven and blend half the drippings into the corn meal mixture. Pour into the hot pan and bake for 15 minutes. Cut into wedges or squares to serve.

SOUTHERN CORNSTICKS

Makes 16

⅔ cup sunflower oil
1 cup self-rising corn meal
1 cup buttermilk
1 large egg
2 Tbsp sunflower oil
1 tsp sea salt

Preheat the oven to 500°F. Put 1½ teaspoons of oil in each of the 8 sections of 2 cornstick pans, or 3 teaspoons in each of 8 large muffin pans. Use a pastry brush to coat each entire section with oil. Place the pans in the oven until they are very hot. Combine the corn meal, buttermilk, egg, oil, and salt in a small mixing bowl. Mix with a wire whisk or a fork. The batter will be runny. Remove the hot pans from the oven and fill each section half-full with the cornmeal mixture. Bake the cornsticks for 20 minutes.

HOE CAKES

Makes 8 to 12

Vegetable shortening
1 cup corn meal
1 tsp sea salt
1 cup boiling water

Heat about ¼ inch vegetable shortening in a heavy 9- or 10-inch skillet (cast iron is best), until it is almost smoking. While the oil is heating, mix the corn meal and salt in a bowl. Beat in the boiling water with a spoon until you achieve a thick consistency. Drop from the spoon into grease and fry until golden on the bottom. Turn and fry the other side. Drain on paper towels.

Southern Cornbread

ARTICHOKE AND PASTA SALAD

Serves 6

One 14-oz can artichoke hearts, drained and divided
1 Tbsp olive oil
1 Tbsp water
1 Tbsp fresh lemon juice
$\frac{1}{2}$ tsp dried basil
$\frac{1}{4}$ tsp dried oregano
$\frac{1}{4}$ tsp black pepper
1 clove garlic, chopped
3 cups cooked radiatori or other pasta shapes
2 cups thin sliced spinach
1 cup plum tomatoes, seeded and chopped
Basil leaves, to garnish
$\frac{1}{4}$ cup crumbled feta cheese

Combine two of the artichoke hearts with the olive oil, water, lemon juice, basil, oregano, black pepper, and garlic in a blender or food processor fitted with a steel blade and process until smooth.

Coarsely chop the remaining artichoke hearts and combine with the pasta, spinach, and chopped tomato in a large bowl. Pour the puréed artichoke mixture over the pasta mixture and toss well to coat.

Cover and chill for 2 hours. Sprinkle with basil leaves and feta cheese to serve.

Artichoke and Pasta Salad

RED BEAN AND RICE SALAD

Serves 8 to 10

2 cups cooked small red beans
1 cup cooked long-grain rice
1 cup celery, sliced thin, with leaves
1 cup diced onions
1 cup seeded and diced plum tomatoes
½ cup seeded and diced green bell peppers
4 cloves garlic, minced

FOR THE DRESSING

⅓ cup bottled Italian salad dressing
2 Tbsp water
2 Tbsp white vinegar
1 tsp sea salt
½ tsp fresh ground black pepper
½ tsp fresh oregano leaves
½ tsp cayenne
¼ tsp fresh thyme leaves

Combine the red beans, rice, celery, onions, tomatoes, green bell pepper, and garlic in a large bowl and blend gently. In another bowl combine the dressing, water, vinegar, salt, pepper, oregano, cayenne, and thyme and mix well. Pour the dressing over the red bean mixture and toss gently to coat. Cover and chill for about 1 hour to allow the flavors to develop.

PICKLED CABBAGE

Serves 6 to 8

1/3 cup sea salt or pickling salt
1 1/3 cups boiling water
12 banana peppers, stemmed,
   seeded, and cored
1 cup cane sugar
3 Tbsp white vinegar
3 Tbsp cold water
1/2 tsp sea salt
6 cups shredded green cabbage
1 1/4 cups water
1/2 cup white vinegar
1 to 3 tsp crushed red peppers
1 Tbsp grated lemon zest
1/2 tsp sea salt
1/2 tsp fresh ground black pepper or
   white pepper

This recipe needs some forethought since it should stand for 2 to 3 days. In a medium heatproof bowl, combine 1/3 cup salt with the boiling water, dissolving the salt. Allow to cool. Add the peppers to the brine and cover with a plate to keep them submerged. Allow to stand overnight at room temperature. In a large bowl, combine 1/2 cup sugar, 3 tablespoons vinegar, 3 tablespoons cold water, and 1/2 teaspoon salt. Add the shredded cabbage and toss to coat evenly, cover, and allow to stand for 45 minutes.

Drain the cabbage and peppers, discarding the pickle and brine. Thin slice the peppers crosswise.

Add the remaining sugar, water, vinegar, crushed red peppers, lemon zest, salt, and pepper to a large saucepan. Bring to a boil, stirring constantly until a syrup forms, about 3 to 4 minutes. Add the cabbage and peppers and cook for 2 to 3 minutes. If you want a sharp pickle add more vinegar to taste. Pack in pickle jars or a large sealing bowl and refrigerate for 2 to 3 days before serving.

SUNFLOWER SLAW

Serves 6 to 8

1/2 cup sunflower seeds
1/2 cup sliced almonds
1 cup Ramen noodles
1/2 cup seasoned rice vinegar
1 cup cane sugar
1 Tbsp soy sauce
1/2 to 1 cup sunflower oil
1 large Napa cabbage, shredded
6 scallions, sliced thin
1 cup shredded sweet red pepper

Place the sunflower seeds on a cookie sheet and toast. Place the almonds on another cookie sheet and toast until golden brown, taking care not to burn. Crumble the Ramen noodles onto a cookie sheet and toast until just browned. Combine in a bowl and reserve.

Combine the rice vinegar, sugar, and soy sauce and heat to dissolve the sugar. Allow to cool. When cool combine the oil and vinegar mixture with a wire whisk.

In a large serving bowl combine the cabbage, onions, and peppers and toss to blend. Cover and chill.

Do not assemble the salad until you are ready to serve it. To serve, pour the cooled dressing over the slaw, sprinkle the toasted mixture over the salad, and toss well.

Green Bean and New Potato Salad

Serves 10 to 12

2 lb new potatoes, scrubbed
   and rinsed
1 Tbsp sea salt
1 lb fresh green beans, trimmed
1 Tbsp sea salt
¼ cup mint leaves, minced
¼ cup chives, minced
2 Tbsp fresh parsley, minced
1 Tbsp fresh thyme leaves, minced
¼ cup extra-virgin olive oil
Juice of 1 lemon
1 Tbsp grated lemon zest
1 tsp sea salt
1 tsp fresh ground black pepper

Add the potatoes to a large stockpot with 1 tablespoon salt and cover by 2 inches with water. Cook, covered, for 10 to 15 minutes or until the potatoes are just tender. Place 1 quart water and 1 tablespoon salt in another stockpot and bring to a boil. Add the green beans, cover, and cook until tender but still crisp, 4 to 5 minutes. Drain the potatoes and beans in a colander. Place in a large bowl. In a small bowl combine the mint, chives, parsley, thyme, oil, lemon zest, salt, and pepper and blend well. Pour over the warm potato and bean mixture and gently toss, coating well. Chill or serve warm.

Pecan Pie

Serves 8 to 10

½ cup dark corn syrup
1 cup cane sugar
½ stick butter, melted
3 large eggs, beaten to bright yellow
1¼ cups pecan halves
One 9-in unbaked pie pastry shell

Preheat the oven to 400°F.

In a medium mixing bowl, combine the syrup, sugar, and butter and mix well. Add the eggs and pecans and blend in. Fill the unbaked pie shell with the mixture. Bake for 10 minutes in the middle of the oven. Reduce the heat to 350°F and continue baking for 30 to 35 minutes, until set around the edges. The pie will not be completely set in the middle when done. Cool before serving.

Pecan Cookies with Peaches and Cream

Serves 10 to 15

1¼ cups pecans
1¼ sticks butter
6 Tbsp cane sugar
1½ cups flour
½ tsp sea salt
Confectioner's sugar (optional)

FOR THE FILLING

1 cup heavy cream, whipped
1 tsp vanilla
2 tsp cane sugar
1 to 2 cups fresh ripe peaches or
    other fruit in season, sliced
Additional whipped cream (optional)
Confectioner's sugar (optional)

Preheat the oven to 375°F.

Brown the nuts in the oven for 5 to 10 minutes, taking care they do not burn. Cool then chop them in a grater or food processor until they are fine, but not a powder. Cream the butter and sugar together. Sift the flour with the salt, add the nuts, and stir into the creamed mixture to make a smooth dough. Divide into 3 equal pieces and shape into flat rounds. Place each between 2 sheets of waxed paper and chill for 30 minutes or until firm. Roll or pat out into ⅛ inch thick rounds. Refrigerate if hard to handle. Remove the top layer of paper and cut into small 2 or 3-inch rounds with a cookie cutter. Bake on a cookie sheet for 10 minutes or until the edges begin to brown. Be careful not to overbake. They will be soft when done and will harden as they cool. Remove them from the cookie sheet to a cooling rack. Cool.

Store, covered, at room temperature or in a freezer. One hour before serving, whip the cream with vanilla and sugar. Sandwich the whipped cream and peaches between two cookies. Immediately before serving, decorate the top with additional whipped cream or sprinkle with confectioner's sugar.